QUICK AND E...

Decorating with Dried Flowers

JILL THOMAS

WARD LOCK

A WARD LOCK BOOK

First published in the UK 1995
by Ward Lock
Wellington House
125 Strand
London
WC2R 0BB

A Cassell Imprint

Distributed in the United States
by Sterling Publishing Co., Inc.
398 Park Avenue South, New York, NY 10016-8810

Distributed in Australia
by Capricorn Link (Australia) Pty Ltd
2/13 Carrington Road, Castle Hill NSW 2154

A British Library Cataloguing in Publication Data block for this book may
be obtained from the British Library

ISBN 0-7063-7345-6

Typeset by Litho Link Ltd, Welshpool, Powys, Wales
Printed and bound in Spain by Graficromo, S.A., Cordoba

ACKNOWLEDGEMENTS
With thanks to Teresa King for her help and advice.

PHOTOGRAPH ACKNOWLEDGEMENTS
Photographs courtesy of:
Camera Press/Avotakka 37; **Camera Press/Brigitte** 36, 56; **Camera
Press/Fuer Sie** 69; **Camera Press/Kotiliesi** 44, 45, 64, 68, 76; **House
& Interiors** 9, 32, 33, 40, 41, 49, 52, 53, 57, 60, 61, 65, 72, 73, 77,
80, 81, 84, 85; **Ward Lock** 4, 13, 17, 20, 21, 28, 48, 88.

contents

Few things can transform the appearance of a room more quickly and easily than flowers. Fresh flowers, though lovely, are ephemeral. Dried flowers – beautiful, versatile and long-lasting – can make the transformation permanent. Their soft, subtle colours and varied shapes and textures lend themselves to a wide range of decorative styles, and their distinctive charm gives them a place in every home. Easy to handle and needing neither light nor water, dried flowers offer a unique combination of qualities and design possibilities. This opens up an exciting range of options for the home decorator.

People have been decorating their homes with dried flowers and herbs for centuries, but the range of material available to the dried-flower designer is now wider than ever before. Specialist shops and suppliers offer a wealth of both home-grown and exotic flowers, seedheads, leaves, cones, pods, grasses, lichen and fungi, plus all the equipment needed to arrange them.

It has never been easier to put together stunning dried-flower decorations that will add colour and interest to your home all year round, and it need be neither time-consuming nor expensive – especially if you are able to grow and dry some of the flowers for yourself.

DECORATING WITH DRIED FLOWERS

Dried flowers have a place in every room in the house. Because they do not require light or water, they are ideal for areas where fresh flowers and plants would not survive. In fact, bright sunlight and excessive moisture are positively harmful to dried plants, eventually causing colours to fade and petals to droop.

The first thing to consider when planning a dried-flower decoration is where it will be placed. If it is to be positioned in the hall, for example, where it will rarely receive more than a passing glance, it will need to make an immediate impact. If in the kitchen or living room, on the other hand, where it will be seen for longer periods, it can be more restrained in style, harmonizing with the room rather than forcing itself on your attention.

Then think about the style of room the flowers will decorate. A formal dining room with polished mahogany table and chairs, for example, would call for a very different type of flower decoration to a family kitchen filled with painted pine or limed oak. A living room that is all modern furniture, uncluttered lines and muted colours would demand a different approach to a cosy, countrified room full of faded chintzes and old rugs.

Halls

Make first impressions count by using dried flowers to create a welcoming display in your entrance hall. This important area is often neglected, but even the tiniest hall usually has room for some form of dried-flower decoration – if there is no space on a side table or for a free-standing arrangement on the floor, use the walls for hanging space or even suspend a big globe of dried flowers from the ceiling.

Here you can go for a really bold arrangement, such as a collection of large, interestingly shaped seedheads and grasses or, for a dark hall, a cheerful mix of orange, red and yellow flowers. Equally striking would be a cool, airy arrangement in white and silver, backed by a mirror to double its effect.

Living rooms

Resist the temptation to decorate every surface in the living room with dried flowers. If you are not careful, you can end up with a confusing muddle of small arrangements on windowsills, side tables and bookcases, and hanging on the walls and backs of doors. A couple of large, well-chosen arrangements will be far more effective. In summer, a basket of flowers might fill the fireplace; in winter, a dramatic swag or garland will enliven the chimney breast. A pedestal arrangement or a good-sized flower tree might be ideal for an alcove or for that awkward dark corner. A big, beautiful bouquet of dried flowers could be a striking permanent feature on a side table or cupboard.

The flower colours can co-ordinate or contrast with the room's colour scheme. For example, warm browns, oranges and golds in the dried flowers would look good with creams and beiges, peach and apricot shades with blues, and pinks and reds with greens. For a more subtle approach, pick out one or two basic colours from curtains, carpets or upholstery fabric and use them again in the flowers, perhaps in a deeper tone or wider range of shades.

Kitchens and bathrooms

Kitchens and bathrooms must be well ventilated if dried flowers are to last long, otherwise the moisture can easily spoil them.

Informal country-style arrangements look good in most kitchens. The simplest are bunches of garden flowers and seedheads or herbs such as dill, rosemary and sage hung from the ceiling to dry. Or you could follow a culinary theme, using maize cobs, dried fungi, heads of garlic, sheaves of wheat, oats and barley, and brightly coloured gourds.

In the bathroom, hang arrangements on the wall or keep them on shelves where they will not be splashed by water. Scented flowers such as lavender or roses are especially appropriate here, as are pretty jars or bowls filled with pot-pourri. The colours can echo the bathroom colour scheme, picking out the colours of towels, carpet or curtains.

Bedrooms

Bedrooms are ideal places for dried-flower decorations, which can bring even the simplest interior to life. Flowered swags look charming around mirrors, over bedheads, along pelmets or even as curtain tie-backs. Wreaths will give a lift to dull wardrobe or cupboard doors.

Dried flowers for bedrooms should be pretty and light, never too grand or heavy. Victorian-style posies and miniature baskets of flowers can be placed on bedside tables or chests of drawers, and a small bouquet in a delicate porcelain vase on the dressing table. Keep both shapes and colours fresh and simple, perhaps using the colours and patterns of your curtains or bedlinen as a starting point.

Designing with dried flowers means making the most of their subtle and varied colours, fascinating range of shapes and unique textures. It also means thinking about where an arrangement will be placed, what kind of container it will need, the angle from which it will be seen, and the style and colours of the room for which it is intended.

When planning dried-flower arrangements, remember that dried flowers are not simply substitutes for fresh flowers. Make the most of their special qualities. Take advantage of the versatility that makes them perfect as long-lasting decorative features in a host of different situations throughout the home.

COLOUR

As flowers dry, their colours tend to fade and soften, so the colours of most dried flowers are naturally more muted and subtle than those of fresh ones. There are exceptions, of course – the brilliant orange of physalis, the deep reds and pinks of some helichrysums, the bright yellow of achillea – but even these cannot compare with the vibrancy of, say, a scarlet rose.

The dried flowers with the brightest colours of all are those which have been dyed. These are readily available, but should be used with care as their colours are often crude and harsh, jarring with the gentler shades of naturally coloured dried flowers. They can, however, come into their own if a special shade is needed to tie an arrangement into a particular colour scheme, or to give life to dull material.

The muted colours of dried flowers make the use of colour in dried-flower design relatively straightforward, and you are unlikely to have to worry about violently clashing colours. Instead, you will need to guard against the monotonous effect of too many similar shades.

The theory of colour effects is usually expressed as a 'colour wheel'. The colours on the wheel run from red through orange to yellow, green, blue, purple and back to red again. Colours that are close together on the colour wheel – yellow and green, blue and purple, red and orange and so on – are *toning* colours. When arranged together, they should be harmonious and easy on the eye, though an arrangement in subdued toning colours may also be dull. The liveliest effects come from mixing colours that are opposite each other on the colour wheel, such as red and green, yellow and purple, or blue and orange. These are *contrasting* colours and they create strong, vibrant mixes. To try out the effect of colour contrast, add a few red flowers

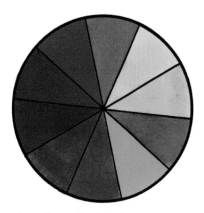

The colour wheel. Colours opposite each other on the wheel are contrasting colours. Colours close together are toning colours.

Dried flower shapes range from the flat heads of achillea and the circles of honesty pods to the spires of amaranthus.

to an arrangement that is made up mostly of blues and greens, and notice how it immediately takes on a more dynamic look.

Whites, creams and silvers are very useful in dried-flower designs. Not only can they look very effective on their own – think of the impact of a huge bunch of airy white gypsophila heads – but they also have a cooling and softening effect when used with brighter colours. The quick-reference table on pages 15–16 groups dried flowers by colour to help you select appropriate material for your designs.

Do not be afraid to experiment with colour, because the most exciting results often come from being too bold rather than too timid. Above all, do not be afraid to follow your own tastes, whatever the rules say, because in the end it is what pleases *your* eye that is most important.

SHAPE

Traditional fresh-flower arrangements take advantage of the pleasing contrast between a formal basic design and the softness and suppleness of the living material used to carry it out. This contrast is harder to achieve with dried flowers, because of their stiffness and inflexibility.

Dried plant material does not fall naturally into the attractive shapes taken by fresh flowers and leaves: stems do not curve, nor leaves and petals droop softly. The qualities of dried flowers are quite different: stems are rigid, shapes are bolder and more geometric. Flowerheads are in flat planes, like achillea and statice, circles, like honesty seedpods or helichrysum, or spires like amaranthus and larkspur. They do not move about or change shape or colour (except to fade slightly with age), but stay in place indefinitely.

Current trends in dried-flower design make a virtue of these qualities. Instead of trying to imitate fresh-flower arrangements, dried flowers are used to create blocks of colour and bold geometric designs that would be impossible with fresh material (for examples, see pages 40 and 72). There will always be a place for the traditional

Achillea

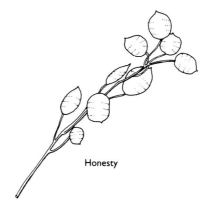

Honesty

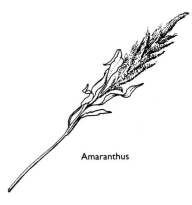

Amaranthus

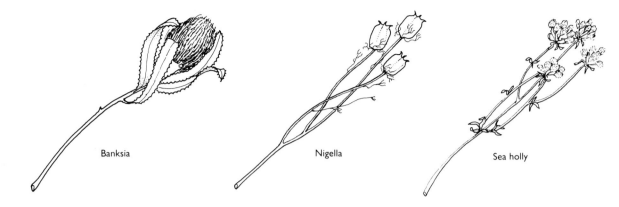

Banksia

Nigella

Sea holly

Dried plants such as banksia, nigella and sea holly offer exciting textures that can be used to give variety to a design.

arrangement, of course, and there are many beautiful examples throughout this book, but much can be learnt from the newer styles. Traditional or modern, however, the best results are always achieved when you take a simple shape as the starting point – it could be a circle, semi-circle, triangle, fan or rectangle. Then, as you fill out the design, think carefully about the individual shapes of the material you are using, balancing round, flat, pointed, curved, soft and hard outlines to give depth and character.

Simple shapes to use as the starting point for dried-flower designs include the circle, the semi-circle, the triangle and the fan.

TEXTURE

Texture is as important as shape in dried-flower design, and the two should work very closely together. Dried flowers and plants offer an immense range of different textures, from the fluffy heads of grasses to the tightly packed florets of achillea, from the stiff rows of grains in an ear of wheat to the crinkled curves of statice, from the shiny, papery petals of many everlastings to the smooth opaqueness of hydrangeas. Especially dramatic are some of the exotics from South Africa and Australia, such as banksia (Australian honeysuckle) with its big, brush-shaped heads, or the giant, daisy-like proteas. Then there are seedheads, from the delicate, spiky pods of nigella to huge drumstick-shaped alliums, big bold cardoons, prickly sea holly, cones of all kinds – the list could go on and on.

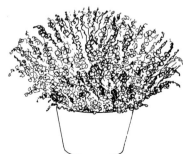

Use the variety of dried-plant textures to add surface interest to your design. Mix flat with spiky, fluffy with smooth, closely packed heads with open, airy ones, small petals with large, to create the exciting rhythm that gives each arrangement its own special character.

CREATING AN ARRANGEMENT

When planning a dried-flower arrangement, think first about where it is to go. Is the room dominated by any strong colours or shapes? What is the style of decoration? Is the room light or dark? Will the arrangement be placed on the floor, a table, a wall? Will it be seen from the side, from above, from below, from all round? The answers to these questions will dictate the style, colour, size and shape of your design.

This bold arrangement uses a well-chosen mix of shapes and textures.

Free-standing arrangements

The most effective free-standing arrangements are based on very simple shapes and achieve their effect through the colours, shapes and textures of the plant material used. The choice of container can have an important bearing on the design – for example, a shallow porcelain bowl might be filled with a low, smoothly mounded arrangement, while a large wicker basket could contain an exuberant mass of grasses and flower spikes spilling out in all directions.

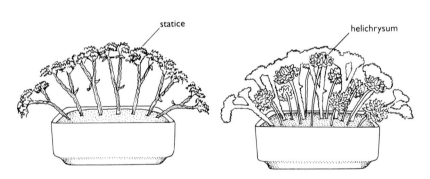

statice

helichrysum

| 1 | The easiest way to build up any arrangement is to create a framework with the tallest items you are using, which might be grasses, flower spikes or sprays of leaves. Before doing this, decide on the angle from which the design will be seen. If it is to be viewed from all sides, make the centre the highest point of the arrangement. If it is to be seen from one side only, the highest point should be at the back.

2 Then use the rest of the material to build up around the framework until you are satisfied with the design.

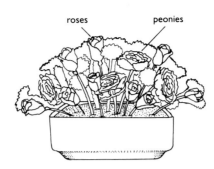

roses   peonies

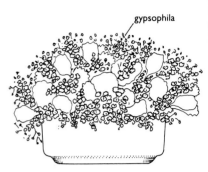

gypsophila

[3] Position the flowers in blocks of colour and texture for best effect, especially in larger designs, and make use of the same flowers at different heights within the design to create a rhythm.

[4] If you do not want to make the mass of flowers too solid, use fluffy seedheads and grasses and open-textured flowerheads, such as gypsophila or alchemilla, to soften the effect.

Never be mean with the flowers unless you are deliberately aiming for a very restrained look. More often than not, dried flowers look best when used with a generous hand and, especially at first, it is far better to use plenty of everyday flowers than just a few choice and expensive rarities.

Posies and miniatures

Dried flowers are ideal for small-scale arrangements of all kinds, from Victorian-style posies to tiny baskets and vases of flowers. Posies are ideal decorations for the bedroom – their formal, old-fashioned charm seems to fit in especially well – and miniature arrangements are often just right for places where space is limited, such as on a dressing table or bathroom shelf.

Posies are traditionally made up of tightly packed rings of flowers arranged around a single, central bud. Dried rosebuds are ideal for posies, with perhaps cornflowers and daisy-like flowers such as helichrysums or anaphalis, edged with something frothy like alchemilla, gypsophila or delicate green leaves. Use flowers in contrasting or toning colours and aim to create a flat, round head, with each circle of colour crisply defined. For a truly Victorian effect, finish the posy with a lacy paper doily and trim with matching ribbon.

When making miniature arrangements, make sure that the material that you are using is in the same scale as the size of arrangement, or the final effect will be clumsy. Use flowers with small heads, or pull larger flowerheads apart into separate florets. Wire these individually

A posy arrangement has a formal, old-fashioned charm.

Pretty eggcups and tiny baskets make ideal containers for miniature arrangements.

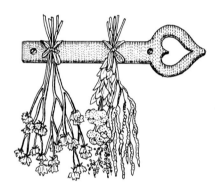

Hanging bunches are a simple and very effective way of displaying dried flowers.

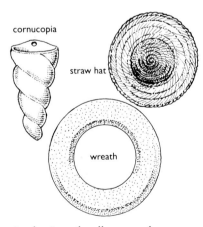

cornucopia

straw hat

wreath

A selection of wall-mounted displays.

if necessary (see pages 22–24). Suitable containers for miniature arrangements include tiny baskets, bud-vases, and small, pretty pieces of china such as eggcups, coffee cups and saucers, or fingerbowls. To secure flowers in small containers, wedge or glue a tiny piece of dry foam in the bottom, or stick a piece of plasticine inside.

Wall and ceiling arrangements
Dried flowers are ideal for wall- and ceiling-mounted arrangements. These can be used almost anywhere in the house, creating plenty of impact while taking up very little space. They can range from something as simple as a bunch of flowers or a sheaf of wheat hung from a nail in the wall to a long, complicated swag or garland using many different materials and draped over a chimney breast or along the banisters.

There is a wide range of containers available designed to be filled with dried flowers and mounted on the wall. These include wicker baskets, hampers, cornucopias, flat-backed pottery or porcelain bowls, mirrored planters and many more. Wreaths of dry foam, wired moss or vines, straw hats and fans, and ropes of plaited straw or raffia are also popular starting points for dried-flower designs. Instead of buying commercially made bases for wreaths, ropes, swags and garlands, it is surprisingly easy to make your own – see page 26 for details.

When designing a hanging arrangement of any kind, think carefully about its positioning. If it is placed too high up the full effect may be lost. If too low, it may be knocked or damaged.

Table decorations
Flowers are traditional at the dinner table, and a carefully thought-out arrangement always lends a sense of occasion to a special meal. One very practical advantage to dried-flower table decorations is that once you have created the arrangement there is no reason why it should not be used for several sets of dinner guests.

Depending on the size of your dining table, table decorations could include a single centrepiece, or perhaps more than one for a really long table, together with tiny individual arrangements for each place setting. The centrepiece should be low enough for people to see over the top – no one wants to have to peer through a mass of vegetation to talk to their opposite number during a meal.

Stick to a single theme: the dominant colour could be suggested by the table linen, china, or colour scheme of the room. The smaller arrangements should follow the centrepiece in style – ideally, use the same colour range for the dried flowers and smaller versions of the same container. If you have room, add another, complementary arrangement for a sideboard, side table or mantelpiece.

DRIED FLOWERS FOR THE DECORATOR

There is a vast range of flowers, leaves, grasses and seedheads available to the dried-flower designer. The listings below give a selection of the most useful and readily available material. The plants are grouped by colour, as this is likely to be the most important factor in choosing material for any design.

For further details of plants suitable for drying, see Flowers and Plants for Drying, pages 89–91.

spp. = species

Pink
Achillea millefolium 'Cerise Queen' (yarrow)
Acroclinum roseum (sunray)
Allium spp. (ornamental onion)
Althea rosea (hollyhock)
Arctotis grandis (African daisy)
Astilbe × arendsii (astilbe)
Astrantia major (masterwort)
Banksia spp. (Australian honeysuckle)
Calluna vulgaris (heather)
Centaurea cyanus (cornflower)
Delphinium consolida (larkspur)
Delphinium elatum (delphinium)
Gomphrena globosa (globe amaranth)
Helichrysum bracteatum (strawflower)
Helipterum manglesii (Swan River daisy)
Heuchera spp. (coral flower)
Hydrangea macrophylla (mophead hydrangea)
Limonium sinuatum (statice)
Nigella damascena (love-in-a-mist)
Paeonia spp. (peony)
Protea spp.
Rosa spp. (rose)
Salvia horminum (clary)
Xeranthemum annuum (everlasting flower)

Red
Acer spp. (maple: leaf)
Acroclinum roseum (sunray)
Amaranthus caudatus (love-lies-bleeding)
Amaranthus paniculatus
Arctotis grandis (African daisy)
Astilbe × arendsii (astilbe)
Atriplex hortensis (orach)
Callistemon citrinus (bottlebrush)
Celosia argentea cristata (cockscomb)
Celosia plumosa

Delphinium elatum (delphinium)
Euphorbia griffithii 'Fireglow' (spurge)
Helichrysum bracteatum (strawflower)
Heuchera spp. (coral flower)
Hydrangea macrophylla (mophead hydrangea)
Paeonia spp. (peony)
Rosa spp. (Rose)

Orange
Acer spp. (maple: leaf)
Arctotis grandis (African daisy)
Carthamus tinctorius (safflower)
Celosia plumosa
Helichrysum bracteatum (strawflower)
Physalis franchetii (Chinese lantern: seedpod)

Yellow
Acacia spp. (mimosa, wattle)
Achillea filipendulina 'Gold Plate' (yarrow)
Alchemilla mollis (lady's mantle)
Althea rosea (hollyhock)
Anethum graveolens (dill)
Anigozanthus coccineus (kangaroo paw)
Banksia occidentalis (Australian honeysuckle)
Catalpa speciosa (Indian bean tree: seedpod)
Celosia plumosa
Centaurea macrocephala (knapweed)
Craspedia globosa (drumstick)
Helichrysum bracteatum (strawflower)
Limonium sinuatum (statice)
Linum perenne (flax: seedhead)
Lonas inodora (African daisy)

Rosa spp. (rose)
Santolina (cotton lavender)
Solidago (golden rod)
Zea mays (maize, corn)

Green
Amaranthus paniculatus
Ambrosinia mexicana
Astrantia major (masterwort)
Atriplex hortensis (orach)
Avena sativa (oats: grass)
Betula pendula (silver birch: leaf)
Festuca spp. (fescue: grass)
Euphorbia spp. (spurge)
Hakea cucullata (hakea: leaf)
Hordeum vulgare (barley: grass)
Humulus lupulus (hop)
Hydrangea macrophylla (mophead hydrangea)
Laurus nobilis (bay: leaf)
Molucella laevis (bells-of-Ireland)
Nicandra physaloides (shoo-fly plant)
Phalaris canariensis (Canary grass)
Phleum pratense (Timothy grass)
Ruscus aculeatus (butcher's broom: leaf)
Triticum aestivum (wheat: grass)
Viburnum tinus (laurustinus)

Blue
Aconitum napellus (monkshood)
Buddleia davidii (butterfly bush)
Centaurea cyanus (cornflower)
Delphinium consolida (larkspur)
Delphinium elatum (delphinium)
Echinops ritro (globe thistle)
Eryngium spp. (sea holly)
Festuca glauca (blue fescue: grass)
Hydrangea macrophylla (mophead hydrangea)
Limonium sinuatum (statice)
Nigella damascena (love-in-a-mist)

Purple/mauve

Acanthus mollis (bear's breeches)
Allium spp. (ornamental onion)
Buddleia davidii (butterfly bush)
Calluna vulgaris (heather)
Cynara cardunculus (cardoon)
Cynara scolymus (globe artichoke)
Delphinium consolida (larkspur)
Delphinium elatum (delphinium)
Helleborus orientalis (Lenten rose)
Lavandula spica (lavender)
Salvia hormum (clary)
Limonium latifolium (see lavender)
Limonium sinuatum (statice)
Xeranthemum annuum (everlasting flower)

White/cream

Achillea ptarmica 'The Pearl' (yarrow)
Acroclinum roseum (sunray)
Allium spp. (ornamental onion)
Ammobium alatum (winged everlasting)
Anaphalis margaritacea (pearl everlasting)
Anaphalis triplinervis (snowy everlasting)
Arctotis grandis (African daisy)
Astilbe × *arendsii* (astilbe)

Buddleia davidii (butterfly bush)
Centaurea cyanus (cornflower)
Clematis spp. (seedhead)
Cortaderia selbana (pampas grass)
Delphinium consolida (larkspur)
Delphinium elatum (delphinium)
Gomphrena globosa (globe amaranth)
Gypsophila paniculata (baby's breath)
Helichrysum bracteatum (strawflower)
Helipterum manglesii (Swan River daisy)
Helleborus niger (Christmas rose)
Helleborus orientalis (Lenten rose)
Heuchera spp. (coral flower)
Hydrangea macrophylla (mophead hydrangea)
Lagarus ovatus (hare's tail grass)
Limonium latifolium (sea lavender)
Limonium sinuatum (statice)
Nigella damascena (love-in-a-mist)
Paeonia spp. (peony)
Rosa spp. (rose)
Salvia horminum (clary)
Xeranthemum (everlasting flower)

Grey/silver

Artemisia spp.
Cineraria maritima (cineraria: leaf)

Eryngium spp. (sea holly)
Eucalyptus spp. (leaf)
Lunaria annua (honesty: seedpod)
Salvia officinalis (sage: leaf)
Santolina (cotton lavender: leaf)

Brown/beige

Allium spp. (ornamental onion: seedhead)
Avena sativa (oats: grass)
Banksia occidentalis (Australian honeysuckle)
Briza maxima (quaking grass)
Centaurea spp. (knapweed: seedhead)
Cones, various
Cycas revoluta (sago palm)
Dipsacus fullonum (teasel)
Fagus sylvatica (beech: leaf)
Gleditsia tricanthus locust: seedpod)
Hordeum vulgare (barley: grass)
Nelumbo nucifera (lotus: seedpod)
Nigella damascena (love-in-a-mist: seedpod)
Papaver (poppy: seedpod)
Protea compacta (protea)
Quercus robur (oak: leaf)
Scabiosa stellata (paper-moon scabious/starflower)
Triticum aestivum (wheat: grass)
Typha latifolia (bulrush/cat-tail)

2

TOOLS AND MATERIALS

The most important material for any dried-flower arrangement is the flowers themselves, but in order to create your design you will need a certain number of basic tools and materials. These are readily available from dried-flower specialists, craft shops and many florists. Few of the items listed here are expensive, although it is worth investing in a good-quality pair of florist's scissors and some secateurs.

If you decide to dry your own flowers, the basic equipment needed is even simpler. The most important requirement is a dry, airy place, well away from direct light (an airing cupboard or attic, for example). You will also need something to hold your bunches of drying flowers together, something from which to hang them, and perhaps glycerine for preserving leaves and desiccant for drying individual flowerheads.

EQUIPMENT FOR DRIED-FLOWER ARRANGEMENTS

Canes
Light canes can be used to support stems if the flowers have large, heavy heads.

Cutters
You will need:
Florist's scissors with short blades and serrated edges – for cutting stems and thin wire.
Secateurs – for cutting thick, woody stems.
Strong, short-bladed knife – for shaping foam.
Wire cutters – for cutting thick wire and wire mesh.

Foam
Foam is the most usual base for dried-flower arrangements. It is best to use the dry foam specially intended for dried flowers rather than the type that soaks up water. Dry foam comes in several shapes and can easily be cut and shaped with a knife.

Foam anchors and fixatives
You will need:

Florist's spikes – plastic or metal spikes or prongs (sometimes called 'frogs') used to secure pieces of foam into a container.

Florist's clay – used to secure either the florist's spike or the foam itself to the base of a container. Plasticine is an alternative.

Clear glue – used as a fixative for foam in permanent arrangements. It may also be needed to glue plant material to a base or into a container. The most efficient method of gluing is to use a hot-glue gun. While this is by no means an essential tool, it can be very useful if you plan to make a lot of large arrangements such as swags, wreaths or garlands that will require glued material.

Table cover
Dried flowers may shed as you are working with them, so it is a good idea to cover your work surface with an old sheet or tablecloth or a piece of oilcloth to catch the debris and prevent mess.

Tape
Florist's tape is a rubber-based adhesive tape, available in brown and green. It is used to bind stems that have been wired to give them a natural look, and can also be used instead of wire to bind bunches of soft-stemmed flowers together. Florist's tape is also invaluable for binding blocks of foam together to fill large containers, and for taping foam into place.

Weights
Dried-flower arrangements sometimes need to be weighted, as they can be top heavy and prone to falling over, especially if the container is only a light basket. Depending on the size of the container, smooth stones, pebbles or marbles can be placed in the bottom to act as weights. For very large arrangements, use a brick or two.

Equipment for dried-flower arrangements.

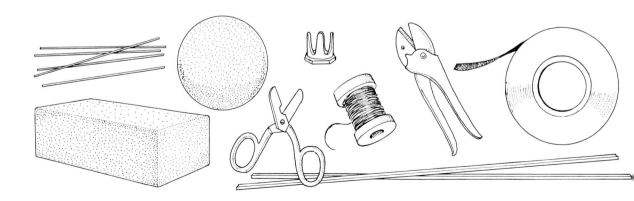

Wire

You will need:

Reel wire – for binding bunches of flowers together and for binding stems.

Rose wire – a thinner version of reel wire, useful for delicate tasks.

Stub wires – used to lengthen, strengthen or replace stems and to give them flexibility. Stub wires come in a variety of lengths from 15cm (6in) to 40cm (16in) and thicknesses from 0.20mm (36swg) to 1.25mm (18swg). The fine- and medium-gauge wires are best for general use.

Wire mesh

Galvanized wire mesh, also known as chicken wire or wire netting, is a very good base for larger arrangements, especially where there is a big container to be filled. It can also be used to cover blocks of foam where extra support is needed for heavy material, and to roll around dried moss as a base for a wreath or swag. Wire mesh with small holes can also be used on its own as a swag base. The most useful sizes are from 1.5cm (½in) to 5cm (2in) mesh, available from most DIY stores, hardware shops and garden centres.

EQUIPMENT FOR DRYING FLOWERS

Canes

Bamboo canes can be hung from the ceiling to make a frame from which to suspend drying bunches of flowers.

Desiccants

Alum, borax, silica gel and silver sand are all desiccants which can be used to dry individual flowerheads.

Glycerine

Glycerine solution is used to preserve both deciduous and evergreen foliage. Antifreeze is an alternative.

Elastic bands

Use these to hold bunches of flowers together while they are drying.

String and wire

These will be needed for making up bunches of flowers to be dried, and for hanging them up.

Wire mesh

Wire mesh is useful for supporting heavy-headed flowers that need to be dried upright.

3

CONSTRUCTION TECHNIQUES

A number of straightforward techniques are required in order to construct attractive and successful dried flower arrangements.

PREPARING THE CONTAINER

Careful preparation of the container is the first step to a successful dried-flower arrangement. It will save time and trouble at a later stage if the arrangement has a secure base made from suitable material.

Foam is the most popular base, as it is soft enough to be easily pierced, holds stems firmly in position and can be cut to whatever shape you need with a sturdy knife. Use the grey-green dry foam specially intended for dried-flower arrangements.

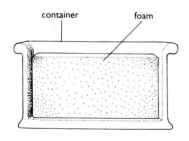

1 The foam must be held securely in the container. With some containers it is possible to cut the foam to size and wedge it in position.

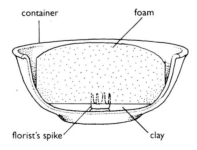

2 With others the foam must be fixed to the base of the container using glue (for permanent arrangements) or a flower spike attached to the base with florist's clay or plasticine.

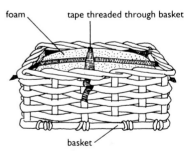

3 If the container is a basket, secure the foam using florist's tape threaded through the woven sides and over the block.

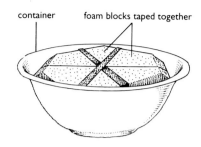

container | foam blocks taped together

container | foam

newspaper

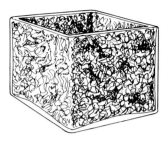

4 Large or wide-mouthed containers such as bowls or baskets may need more than one foam block to fill them. In this case it is best to cut the blocks to shape and then tape them together with florist's tape before fixing them in position.

5 In order to avoid filling a large or deep container with expensive foam, crumpled newspaper can be used as a base and a layer of foam then wedged on top of it. An alternative filling for big containers, especially those with awkward shapes, is crumpled wire mesh.

6 It is important that the base does not show when the arrangement is completed. Line glass containers or loosely woven baskets with dried moss or lichen before they are filled. Use a layer of the same material to hide the foam or wire in wide-mouthed or shallow containers.

Painted containers

A splash of paint can transform a cheap container into something very special. You can colour the container to suit the scheme of the room for which it is intended or to match the flowers that you are using in the arrangement. Woven or wooden containers take paint best – or you could even paint a cardboard box such as a shoe box.

Acrylic paint is the easiest type to use, and comes in a huge range of shades. When you have painted the container, you could spray it with a clear lacquer to make sure that it doesn't smudge or smear. If the container is large, or an awkward shape, a better finish is achieved using spray paint rather than a paint brush. Craft paints in spray form are available from most shops selling artist's or craft materials, although sometimes only in a limited range of colours. If you cannot find the shade you want, most car accessory shops sell small cans of car touch-up paint in a good range of deeper and metallic colours.

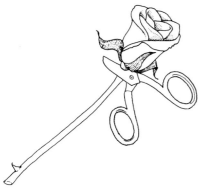

WIRING

Wiring is a very useful technique for the dried-flower arranger. Some flowers are difficult to handle because of fragile or drooping stems, so the stems can be removed and replaced by wires, either before or after drying. Wires can also be used to lengthen short or broken stems, to give stiff stems flexibility and to make false stems for material such as pine cones and maize cobs. In addition, bunches of flowers are often wired together for ease of handling before being incorporated into arrangements.

Wiring before drying

This method is used for fresh flowers, such as roses that are to be dried in desiccant, before drying.

1 Cut off the stem at the base of the flower.

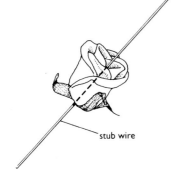

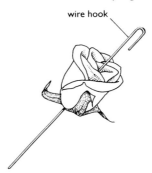

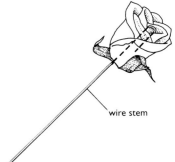

2 Take a medium-gauge (0.71mm/ 24swg) stub wire and push it up through the centre of the base of the flower.

3 Bend the top of the wire over to form an upside-down U shape.

4 Pull the wire back gently so that the U is hooked through the centre of the flower.

Wiring after drying

This method is used for flowers that have been dried on their own stems.

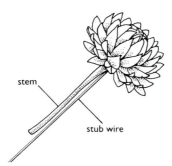

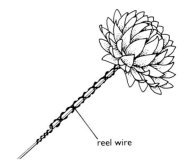

1 Cut off the stem about 5cm (2in) below the flower. Take a medium-gauge (0.71mm/24swg) stub wire and lay it against the stem, touching the base of the flower.

2 Take a length of reel wire and, starting at the base of the stem, bind stem and stub wire together. Go up to the flower base and back down, then tuck in the end of the reel wire .

Wiring a bunch of flowerheads

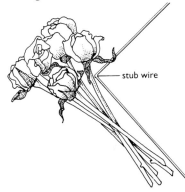

stub wire

1 Take a bunch of five or six flower-heads and arrange them together in the shape you require. Take a medium-gauge (0.71mm/24swg) stub wire and bend it in half to form a right angle. Hold the wire against the flower stems with the free end at right angles to the stems.

2 Wind the free end of the wire downwards around both stems and wire, binding them tightly together. Tuck in the end neatly to leave a single length of wire projecting below the stems.

Wiring cones

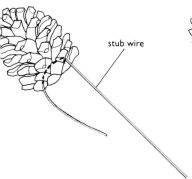

stub wire

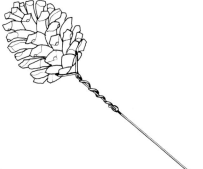

1 The easiest way to give a fir cone a wire stem is to take a medium-gauge (0.71mm/24swg) stub wire and bend one end of it around the base of the cone, above the lowest layer of scales.

2 Pull the wire tight around the cone and twist the ends together to form a stem.

Wiring nuts

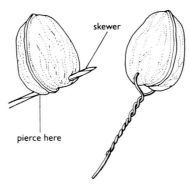

skewer

pierce here

Taping wired stems

1 In order to wire nuts such as Brazil nuts and walnuts for use in dried-flower decorations, the hard shells must be pierced. The best way to do this is to use a heated skewer or an awl, or a very fine drill. The weakest part of the shell is where the two halves join.

Once flower stems have been wired, tape can be used to hide the bare wire. Using a roll of green or brown florist's tape and starting just below the base of the flowerhead, wind the tape firmly around and down the wired stem. Keep the tape pulled tight and smooth as you go to prevent bulges developing.

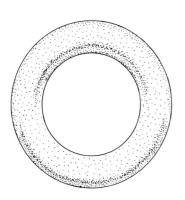

WREATHS

Dried-flower wreaths make very effective decorations, and a wide variety of materials can be used for the bases including dry foam, plaited straw or raffia, vine stems, moss and wire. Ready-made wreath bases of all types can be bought from dried-flower suppliers and florists, but they are also cheap and easy to make.

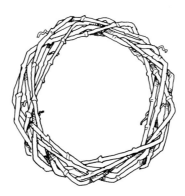

To make a wreath base

The simplest home-made wreath base is constructed from a length of wire mesh rolled around moss. The materials listed are for a medium-sized wreath (diameter 23cm/11in).

There are many different styles of wreath. The base may be thickly covered with flowers, leaves and seedheads, or sections of it may be left undecorated if the base itself is an attractive material such as plaited straw. Depending on the type of base, plant material can be attached either with clear glue or by wiring, pushing the wire firmly into the base and bending it round to secure. Flowers should usually be wired or taped into small bunches before being attached to the wreath.

If possible, hang up the wreath base while you work on it. Ths will enable you to make sure that it is properly covered from all angles.

MATERIALS
PIECE OF WIRE MESH 30 × 90CM
(12 × 36IN) APPROX
DRIED MOSS
REEL WIRE

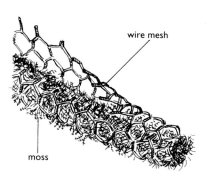

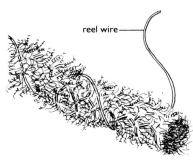

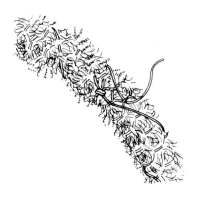

1 Soak the moss briefly in cold water to make it pliable and squeeze out the excess. Lay the length of wire mesh on a flat surface and spread a layer of damp moss along the long edge. Roll the wire firmly around the moss to form a sausage shape.

2 Bind reel wire around the mesh to hold it in place, leaving about 15cm (6in) of reel wire loose at each end.

3 Bend the tube of moss-filled mesh to form a circle. Join the ends of the circle together by threading the loose ends of reel wire through the mesh. This creates an invisible join.

MATERIALS

Swag

PLAITED STRAW OR RAFFIA

OR

PIECE OF 1.5CM (½IN) WIDE
MESH

DRIED MOSS (OPTIONAL)

Garland

REEL WIRE

CORD, RIBBON OR PLAITED
RAFFIA (OPTIONAL)

OR

PIECE OF 1.5CM (½IN) WIRE
MESH

MOSS

SWAGS AND GARLANDS

These are both long constructions of dried flowers and other plant material, designed to be hung or draped. Swags are usually shorter and hung vertically on a door or wall – for example, on either side of a chimney breast. Garlands are longer and often hung in loops.

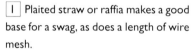

1 Plaited straw or raffia makes a good base for a swag, as does a length of wire mesh.

2 Simple garlands can be made from wired bunches of flowers linked by reel wire or wired on to cord, ribbon or plaited raffia. Heavier garlands, such as Christmas garlands using evergreens and pine cones, will need a more substantial base. Here again, a length of 1.5cm (½in) wire mesh rolled around moss to make a tube may be used. For long garlands, several tubes can be wired together, each tube forming an individual loop.

DRIED-FLOWER TREES

Dried-flower trees can be made in all shapes and sizes. Small trees make ideal decorations for a table, windowsill or mantlepiece; larger, free-standing ones look good in the hall, if there is room, or in a corner of the living room.

The simplest dried-flower trees have round or cone-shaped foam heads, which can be bought ready-cut in a wide range of sizes, with a single piece of wood for the trunk. Flowers, leaves and seedheads, wired or not as necessary, are then inserted directly into the foam to mimic blossom and foliage. It is a good idea to cover the foam with moss before decorating the tree, as this will ensure that no foam can be seen when it is finished.

The trunk is set in a plastic or terracotta flowerpot filled with plaster of Paris to give a solid base. Moss, bark or small pebbles are then used to fill in the top of the pot. For smaller trees, the trunk may be set in foam wedged in the base of the pot and covered with sand or pebbles to give stability.

Multi-trunked trees look very effective. Here, three or four pieces of branch are wired together. The head is fixed on to them, and they are then set in plaster. The wire can then be removed and the tree decorated in the chosen style.

A very simple tree can be made from a well-shaped bare branch. Simply fix the branch firmly into a pot and glue flowers on to the bare twigs of the branch.

MATERIALS

SHAPED PIECE OF DRIED FOAM
PIECE OF WOOD
DRIED MOSS
MEDIUM-GAUGE STUB WIRE
PLASTIC OR TERRACOTTA
FLOWERPOT
PIECE OF GREEN OR BLACK
PLASTIC, CUT TO FIT THE INSIDE
OF THE POT (USE A PIECE OF
GARDEN REFUSE SACK OR BIN
LINER)
FLOWERS, LEAVES AND SEEDHEADS
MOSS, PEBBLES OR BARK

To make a dried-flower tree

1 Push the piece of wood that is to form the trunk firmly into the foam head. Make staples by cutting short pieces of stub wire and bending them into a U shape. Use these to pin the moss to the foam. Line the flowerpot with the plastic.

2 Mix the plaster of Paris powder to a thick paste with water. Hold the trunk in the pot and spoon the mixture around it. Allow to set.

3 Wire the flowers and foliage if necessary. Then push them firmly into the tree head, working all the way round until it is covered. Fill up the pot with moss, bark or pebbles to hide the plastic base.

CONTAINERS

The container is a vital element in any dried-flower design. Its choice can both dictate the style of the arrangement and link it to its surroundings, whether the container is a simply woven basket filled with grasses and seedheads on a kitchen dresser, or a pretty china bowl filled with summer flowers on a living room windowsill.

Containers for dried flowers do not need to be watertight, of course, so there is almost no limit to the items that can be used. You can let your creativity and imagination run riot as you choose from ceramics, wood, basketwork, glass and metal containers in every shape and size. As you look around your home you will probably find there are already many suitable items to hand. Antique and junk shops, and shops selling crafts and ethnic goods, are good places to start looking when you decide to expand your collection.

Woven containers

The natural look of baskets and other woven items is an ideal complement to dried flowers, and woven containers are both relatively cheap and easy to find. Baskets are made all over the world in an enormous variety of shapes and sizes, textures and colours.

All sorts of different materials can be woven into baskets, and each has its characteristic appearance. There are baskets made from bamboo, willow, reeds, palm leaves, hazel, straw and raffia – all with a different tonal range and quality of weave to complement dried flower arrangements in a wide range of styles.

Large baskets are ideal for big arrangements to stand on the floor, in the fireplace or on a side table. Smaller baskets can fit in almost anywhere, and baskets with handles can even be hung from the ceiling if you are short of space.

Many woven items make good wall decorations, too, from flat-backed baskets and cornucopias filled with flowers, through flower-decorated straw and raffia plaits, to straw hats and fans.

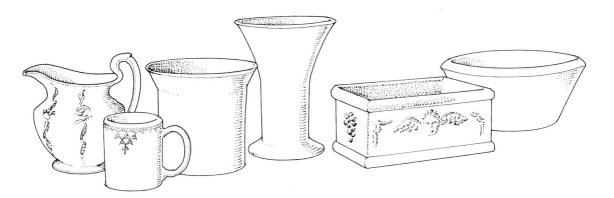

Pottery and porcelain

Pottery and porcelain vases and bowls are classic containers for fresh flowers and can look equally good filled with dried flowers, provided you choose carefully. Often, hand-thrown pottery with its muted earth shades is more in keeping with the colour range of dried flowers than highly decorated china, especially if it has bright colours and gilding. You will not go wrong if you keep to simple shapes, uncluttered designs and plain or soft colours that echo the predominant tones of your arrangement. For large arrangements, the big unglazed terracotta pots and urns designed for garden use can look stunning.

Old china mugs, jugs and bowls often have attractively faded patterns. These can make very effective dried-flower containers and, if chipped or cracked, can often be bought very cheaply.

Glass

Although glass containers are very pretty, they do have the disadvantage that foam bases and stems show through, unless the glass is opaque. If you are using a glass container for a dried-flower arrangement, it is a good idea to line it with moss, lichen or coloured paper before you start. Alternatively, stems and 'mechanics' – the foam, wire mesh and so on used to support plant material – can be

hidden by filling up the container with small pebbles, shavings, pot-pourri, sand or even shells.

As with ceramics, there is a huge range of glass containers from which to choose, but the simplest are usually the most effective. Green and blue glass both go especially well with dried flowers – old glass in these colours is very desirable, but there is a host of cheaper, modern alternatives.

Chunky modern glass vases in shapes such as cubes or globes make splendid containers for understated arrangements in the modern style, and glass ashtrays are often perfect for smaller arrangements.

Wood and metal

Many wooden containers look good filled with dried flowers. Wooden boxes – plain, patterned or lacquered – can be found in many different sizes and are ideal for a wide range of different arrangements, from small to large. They can often be bought very cheaply in craft shops or shops selling ethnic goods. The most widely available wooden bowls are salad bowls, and a collection of these in different sizes and shades of wood would be an excellent starting point for dried-flower decorations for the kitchen and dining room. If you have room, a really big wooden container such as a blanket chest would look splendid filled with a mass of big seedheads, palm fronds and tall grasses.

Metal containers also offer plenty of scope. The soft glow of copper, especially if it is not too brilliantly polished, is wonderful with dried flowers, but brass, pewter and even iron containers are also suitable for use. Apart from metal containers specially designed for flowers and plants, the range of items that could be used includes everything from bowls, mugs and jugs to kitchen equipment such as saucepans, cake tins and jelly moulds.

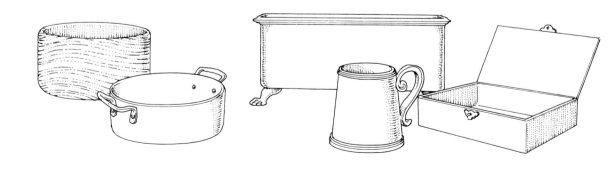

the projects

The pages that follow contain a selection of imaginative projects, with step-by-step instructions, which show just how effectively dried flowers can be used for decoration throughout the home. The projects begin with the simplest and progress through intermediate designs to more elaborate, advanced creations.

kitchen bunches

Big bunches of dried flowers and herbs hanging from the ceiling make a lovely informal decoration for a country-style kitchen, as shown opposite. Air-drying by hanging upside-down is one of the simplest and best ways of preserving many flowers, and – particularly if space is limited – there is no reason not to make a feature of the flowers as they dry.

If your kitchen doesn't offer suitable drying conditions, use ready-dried flowers instead. Mix and match colours and textures to suit your colour scheme, but for the most natural effect try to keep shades muted, and stick to plants that look as though they might have been grown in your own garden. Suitable candidates include lavender, sea holly, sea lavender, achillea, gypsophila, helichrysum, alchemilla, larkspur, the seedheads of poppies and nigella, and herbs such as fennel, dill and rosemary.

Above: An old-fashioned clothes airer that can be raised and lowered with ease is an ideal vehicle for displaying mixed bunches of dried and drying flowers, leaves and seedheads in a country kitchen.

MATERIALS

Hanging frame
8 CUP HOOKS
4 BAMBOO CANES OR LENGTHS
OF DOWELLING, **2M** (**6FT**) LONG
FLEXIBLE WIRE OR STRONG
STRING
RAFFIA
ELASTIC BANDS (OPTIONAL)

PLANT MATERIAL
FLOWERS, SEEDHEADS, HERBS

If you would like to make a feature of flowers as they are drying, you will need to choose a suitable spot for them in order to avoid a disappointing result. Keep the hanging bunches away from direct sunlight and moist air – don't hang them directly over the sink, for example, or close to a window. If you have a solid-fuel cooker your flowers should dry rapidly if hung above it, although not so close as to create a fire hazard. Hanging them above a central-heating boiler would be equally effective. Bunches hung up to dry also need to be well spaced so that air can circulate around them.

Ready-dried flowers are, naturally, less fussy about position, so you can be more adventurous in the way that you place them. You can also pack the bunches more tightly together. Remember to leave plenty of clearance below the flowers if they are hanging over a working area or walkway.

Should you be lucky enough to have exposed beams in your kitchen, the flowers can be attached to wires strung between hooks on the beams. Otherwise, suspend bamboo canes or lengths of dowelling from the ceiling to make a hanging frame. If your ceilings are low, consider attaching the flowers to wall-mounted poles.

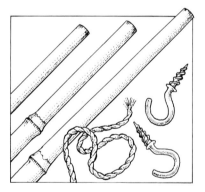

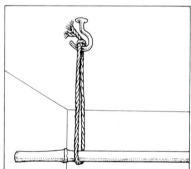

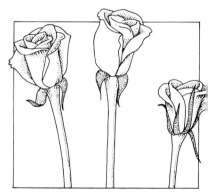

1 Collect together the cup hooks, bamboo canes or dowelling and flexible wire or strong string. Screw a pair of cup hooks into the ceiling, 1.5m (5ft) apart. Repeat at intervals of 30cm (12in) until all hooks have been used.

2 Loop a piece of flexible wire or strong string around the ends of each pole. Use this to suspend the poles from the hooks, making sure that the poles hang at least 15cm (6in) below the ceiling.

3 Select your flowers. If hanging flowers up to dry, make each bunch of the same variety. If using ready-dried flowers, mix and match bunches as you please.

4 Start each bunch by taking five or six of the longest stems. Secure with raffia or an elastic band. (Flowers that are already dry can be wired instead.) Make another two or three small bunches in the same way.

5 Put the bunches together to see how they look. If the effect is too thin, add a few more flowers. Then tie them up with a length of raffia, binding it firmly around the stems.

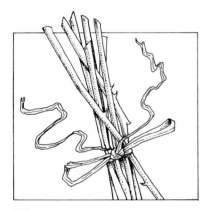

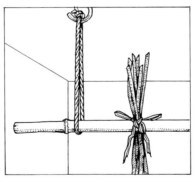

6 Finish off by tying the raffia into a bow. Knot to hold the bow in position, leaving two long ends.

7 Attach the flower bunch to the hanging pole, using the ends of the raffia bow as ties.

8 Repeat until the poles are filled with bunches. Ready-dried flowers can be packed tightly together. Flowers for drying will need to be kept at least 30cm (12in) apart.

hall table

There is no need to spend hours arranging dried flowers in order to create an impact. Even the simplest arrangements can look wonderful if careful thought is given to their placing. In the picture opposite informal bunches in a well-chosen selection of containers decorate an attractive old chest. Tones of rust, cream and blue predominate and these colour harmonies pull together the different elements of the composition.

A grouping such as this, making an immediate impact on the viewer, is just right for a side table in a hall or corridor, or perhaps on a landing. This is an ideal way to make use of any odd or cracked, but still pretty, china jugs, mugs or bowls. The plants used here include helichrysum, gypsophila, hydrangea heads, flax seedheads and fescue grass.

Above: The delicate shades of dried peonies combine with blue-green
eucalyptus leaves in this pretty basket of flowers to make a summery
decoration for a hall or side table.

MATERIALS

Bowl of flowers
LARGE BOWL
DRY FOAM
FLORIST'S TAPE
FLORIST'S SPIKE(S)
FLORIST'S CLAY
SPHAGNUM MOSS OR LICHEN
PLANT MATERIAL
HELICHRYSUM, PINKY RED
GYPSOPHILA, CREAM
HYDRANGEA HEADS, GREEN/PINK
LINUM (FLAX) SEEDHEADS, BROWN
FESCUE GRASS, BROWN

Peony basket
BASKET
PLEATED PAPER RIBBON
WIRE MESH
SPHAGNUM MOSS
PLANT MATERIAL
EUCALYPTUS LEAVES, GREEN
PEONY HEADS, PINK AND CREAM

Choosing and using containers effectively is the key to the grouping on the previous page. Study it for a moment and you will see that the arrangement is not thrown together at random, but linked by both colour and shape. The cool blues of the large jug and bowl, the tan shades of the basket and the cream of the small jugs echo the stripes in the rug and the wood of the chest. The rust, cream and pale browny yellows of the flowers are chosen to harmonize with these shades, with a few soft, pinky red helichrysums to pick up the pattern on the bowl.

The shapes of the flower arrangements are dictated by the shapes of the containers. So a tall, upright container like the big jug contains a tall, upright bunch, while a soft, mounded arrangement reflects the rounded shape of the bowl. The variety of different heights and shapes gives life and interest, but it is important to bear in mind that a mixed grouping like this needs to be linked by a strong and coherent colour theme.

The simplest arrangements of dried flowers and grasses are made in upright, narrow-necked containers like the jug, where they need no support or wiring. Wider arrangements will need some form of support, either dry foam or scrunched-up wire mesh.

1 Wide containers, such as the large bowl shown on the previous page, are usually filled with dry foam to support the flowers. If individual blocks are too small, they can be taped together using florist's tape.

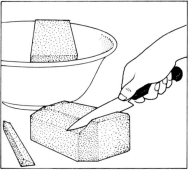

2 Sculpt blocks of foam to fit the inside of the container. The top of the foam should be slightly domed.

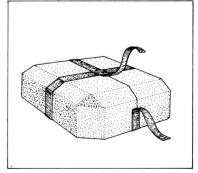

3 Tape the individual blocks of foam together firmly.

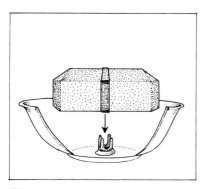

4 Attach one or more florist's spikes (depending on the size of the container) to the base, using florist's clay. Press the taped foam block down firmly on to the spike so that it is held securely in place.

5 Cover the foam with a layer of sphagnum moss or lichen. The moss or lichen should hide the foam blocks completely.

6 Arrange the flowers in the container, pushing the stems well down into the foam. Start in the centre with the tallest items. Work around and down to the sides, remembering that the arrangement will be seen from above as well as from the side. Allow a few flowers to spill over the edge.

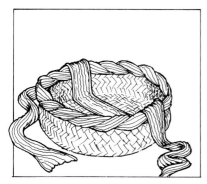

1 **The basket of peonies** is decorated with a length of pleated paper ribbon. Take the ribbon, tease it out slightly and lay it inside the basket with the ends trailing over the sides.

2 Fill the basket with a piece of scrunched-up wire mesh. Cover the wire with a layer of sphagnum moss.

3 Pull up the ends of the ribbon. Arrange the peonies and eucalyptus leaves over and around it, sticking the stems firmly into the wire. To finish, loop the ends of the ribbon over the flowers and tuck down amongst them.

summer baskets

Bring summer colour into the house all year round with a beautiful basket of garden flowers in shades of red, pink and cream, spiked with cool green leaves. Big, bold arrangements such as the one in the main picture are ideal for the living room. This is the focal point in a bay window, but it would look equally at home in an alcove or on a side table. Amongst the plants used are delphiniums, poppies, peonies, statice, amaranthus, hydrangeas, rosebuds and eucalyptus leaves.

Deep pink and red roses in the picture below show how effective a block of colour can be. Although the container is again a woven basket, the mood is far more formal. The mixed flowers make one think of a relaxed setting of stripped pine and pretty floral chintzes; the roses would suit a more modernist interior, perhaps as a splash of colour in a room dominated by creams and neutrals.

Above: Decorate the sitting room with roses and other summer flowers.
This formal arrangement is very effective.

Mixed arrangement
LARGE WICKER BASKET
SMOOTH PEBBLES
NEWSPAPER
SPHAGNUM MOSS (OPTIONAL)
DRY FOAM OR WIRE MESH
FLORIST'S TAPE
PLANT MATERIAL
DELPHINIUMS, PINK
PEONIES, RED AND PINK
STATICE, PINK
AMARANTHUS, DEEP RED
HYDRANGEA HEADS, PINK
ROSEBUDS, RED AND PINK
EUCALYPTUS LEAVES, GREEN
POPPIES, CREAM
Basket of roses
SMALL WICKER BASKET
DRY FOAM OR WIRE MESH
SPHAGNUM MOSS
PALE GREEN PLEATED PAPER
RIBBON
PLANT MATERIAL
2 DOZEN ROSES, RED AND PINK

Baskets seem to have a natural affinity with dried flowers, as the pictures on the previous pages show. Note how the loose weave of the big basket on the table complements the open, relaxed style of the arrangement. The intended impression is that you have just been out into the garden and gathered an armful of flowers. In contrast, the basket containing the roses has a tightly woven, geometric pattern that echoes the tightly packed, upright way in which the flowers are arranged.

Some baskets are very light, and a large arrangement may be top-heavy and liable to tip over. If the basket is deep enough, it is a good idea to weight it with a few smooth pebbles in the bottom. A layer of crumpled newspaper can be placed over the pebbles, with foam wedged on top of the newspaper. This will also avoid you having to fill the basket with expensive foam. Alternatively, crumpled wire mesh could be used.

The baskets shown here are in their natural colours, but they could also be painted in a shade that tones with the colours of the arrangement. The rose basket would look good in deep red, while the mixed basket could be cream or light green. See page 21 for details on painting containers.

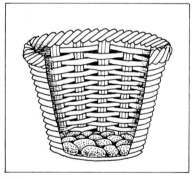

1 **To prepare the large wicker basket** for the mixed arrangement, place a layer of smooth pebbles in the bottom to act as weights.

2 If the basket is a deep one, cover the pebbles with a layer of crumpled newspaper. If the basket has a loose weave through which the newspaper might show, first line the sides with sphagnum moss.

3 Cut blocks of dry foam to shape and wedge them firmly on top of the newspaper. A length of florist's tape, threaded through the sides of the basket, can be used to hold the foam in place.

[4] Select your flowers. The arrangement uses a mix of pink delphiniums, pink hydrangea heads, cream poppies, red and pink rosebuds and peonies, deep red amaranthus, pink statice and eucalyptus leaves.

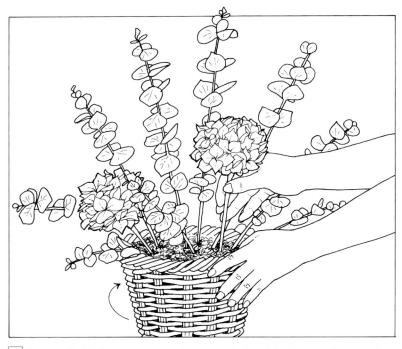

[5] Start to build the arrangement by making a frame with the eucalyptus leaves and statice. Then add the hydrangea heads. Fill in with the remainder of the flowers. Keep turning the basket as you work, so that the arrangement looks equally good from all sides.

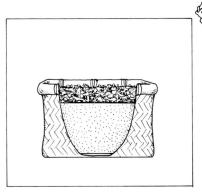

[1] **For the rose arrangement**, fill the basket with blocks of foam or crumpled wire mesh. Cover with sphagnum moss.

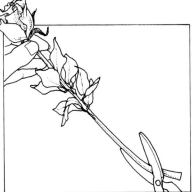

[2] Select two dozen pink and red roses, with leaves, of equal height. Trim stems so that the visible height of the roses is approximately twice the height of the basket.

[3] Arrange the roses in rows in the basket and finish off with a double loop of pale green paper ribbon, tied in a loose knot.

dining-room sideboard

Choose from simply sophisticated or prettily countrified – the arrangements on these pages express two very different moods, but both would be equally at home as decorations in the dining room.
The coolly elegant grouping of matching vases in different sizes, plus a bowl in the same china, shown in the picture opposite, makes a perfect decoration for a sideboard or side table in the dining room. Notice how the three colours combined in the largest vase – white, blue and yellow – are used separately in the smaller arrangements. The yellow apples in the bowl are real: there is no reason why you shouldn't have 'props' such as fresh fruit and vegetables alongside an arrangement of dried flowers.
The clean lines of the vases and the spiky, geometric shape of the large arrangement suggest a room decorated in an uncluttered contemporary style.

Above: The massed flowers in the copper pan suggest a more informal
setting – perhaps the dining room of a cosy cottage.

MATERIALS

Matching vases
3 MATCHED CONTAINERS IN
DIFFERENT SIZES
REEL WIRE
WIRE MESH
FLORIST'S TAPE

PLANT MATERIAL
LARKSPUR, BLUE
CORNFLOWERS, BLUE
AMMOBIUM, WHITE
ACHILLEA, YELLOW

Copper pan of flowers
COPPER PAN
DRY FOAM
FLORIST'S TAPE
SPHAGNUM MOSS

PLANT MATERIAL
AMMOBIUM, WHITE
ACHILLEA PTARMICA, WHITE
HELICHRYSUM, PINK
ACHILLEA MILLEFOLIUM, PINK
ROSEBUDS, RED
CORNFLOWERS, BLUE

A clever use of containers and flower colour is what makes the group of white vases shown on the previous page so effective. Putting together a collection of containers linked by shape and colour, and filling them with flowers in a restricted colour range, is probably the easiest way of all to make a big impact with a limited amount of plant material.

Instead of vases, you could use a whole range of other china or pottery containers. For the dining room, perhaps choose a selection of cups, bowls and jugs from the same tea service, or matching soup bowls and a soup tureen. The flowers need not be restricted to the sideboard or a side table: tiny individual arrangements in coffee cups or even eggcups could decorate each place setting for a dinner party, with a table centrepiece in a larger item of the same china such as a vegetable dish.

The more elegant the china you use, the more sophisticated will be the effect. Keep the flowers themselves simple, especially if your china is heavily patterned. Perhaps pick up just a single colour in the pattern, or a couple of different shades at most.

1 **For the arrangement shown in the main picture** (on page 45), select a range of narrow-necked containers in matching china or pottery.

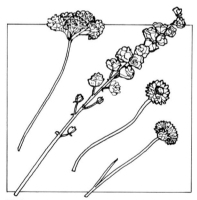

2 The flowers used are blue larkspur and cornflowers, white ammobium (winged everlasting) and yellow achillea.

3 Wire small bunches of ammobium for the large arrangement. Take four or five flower stems and wire them together, starting just below the flowerheads.

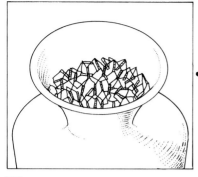

4 Fill the neck of the largest container with a piece of crumpled wire mesh.

5 Starting with a framework of larkspur stems, build up the arrangement with the other flowers.

6 Fill the two smaller container with ammobium and cornflowers respectively. Depending on the shape of your containers, it may be a good idea to wire each bunch first.

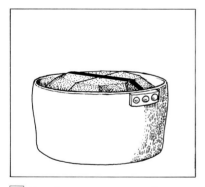

1 **For the copper pan of flowers**, cut blocks of foam to fit the container, mounding them in the centre, and tape them together.

2 Wedge the foam into place and cover it with a layer of moss.

3 Wire together bunches of flowers in pastel shades such as *Achillea ptarmica*, pink helichrysum and ammobium. Working from the centre, fix these into place. Finish with a few individual rosebuds and cornflowers.

fireplace arrangements

Fireplaces lend themselves admirably to being decorated with dried flowers. An inglenook fireplace, as in the picture opposite, suggests a whole range of striking effects. The hop bines and wheat sheaves are reminiscent of autumn and harvest time. They could be replaced by different styles of garland as the seasons change – delicate pastels for spring, brighter colours for summer, pine cones, evergreens and orange physalis for winter.

Above: The sumptuously colourful mass of flowers is a beautiful contrast to
the severity of the dark grey marble fireplace.

Fireplace basket
LARGE BASKET
SMOOTH PEBBLES
SPHAGNUM MOSS
DRY FOAM
FLORIST'S TAPE
STRING
RAFFIA

PLANT MATERIAL
DELPHINIUMS, BLUE
CARTHAMUS, YELLOW
STATICE, ORANGE
HELICHRYSUM, ORANGE/RED
ROSES, ORANGE/PINK
EUCALYPTUS LEAVES, GREEN

Inglenook garland
FLORIST'S TAPE
RAFFIA
STRING

PLANT MATERIAL
OAK LEAVES, BROWN
HOP FLOWERS, GREEN
HOP BINES, GREEN
WHEAT, GREEN

The fireplace arrangement shown on page 48 is very large, but, with patience, it is quite easy to create something of this size using exactly the same techniques as for smaller arrangements. This basket of flowers is designed to be seen from one side only, but you will still need plenty of material – so it is especially suitable if you grow and dry your own flowers. The base of this arrangement is a basket. Other suitable containers for filling a fireplace would be a copper pan (as on page 44), or stoneware or terracotta pots. The flowers used are delphiniums, carthamus, sea lavender, helichrysum, roses and eucalyptus leaves.

Hop bines make attractive garlands on their own, or they can be combined with other plant material, such as the wheat sheaves used here. They can be bought ready dried from good suppliers in lengths of about 2.5cm (9ft). You may need to twist more than one bine together for a full effect. For shorter garlands, the dried stems of other twining plants such as clematis and Russian vine also make a good base, though they will need other additional material as they are far less decorative than hop bines on their own.

1 **For the fireplace basket**, take a large basket and place a few smooth pebbles in the bottom to act as weights.

2 Line the basket with a layer of moss. Cut blocks of dry foam to fit the basket, tape them together and wedge them into place.

3 Make a framework for the arrangement using the eucalyptus leaves, carthamus and delphiniums. The basic shape is that of a fan, with the tallest flowers at the back of the arrangement.

4 Fill in with the remainder of the flowers, working forwards and downwards.

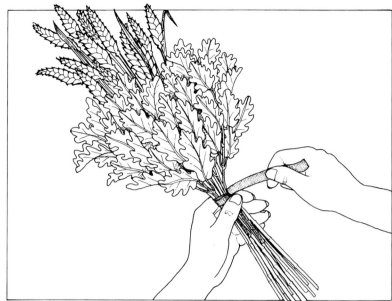

1 **Start the inglenook garland** by making the sheaves. Select a bunch of green wheat and tape it together with florist's tape. Using more tape, attach two branches of oak leaves, preserved in glycerine, to the back of the sheaf.

2 Thread bunches of hop flowers through the tape at the front of the sheaf.

3 Tie a loose raffia bow around the sheaf to hide the tape. Trim the stems.

4 To make the hop garland, twist the ends of lengths of hop bine together and tie with string.

kitchen baskets

Dried flowers look good in most kitchens, but they need to be kept out of the way of working and food storage areas. The neat solution is to hang them up, from the ceiling or on the walls. The picture opposite shows a mixed, informal arrangement that uses an old clothes airer as its base. The centrepiece is a trug filled with hydrangea heads and statice, flanked by hanging bunches. For variations on this theme see pages 32 and 56.
If your kitchen isn't suitable for a hanging arrangement such as this, then mount your dried flowers on the wall. In the picture below, a pine box makes the perfect container for a mix that includes achillea, ammobium, alchemilla, poppy seedheads, hare's tail grass and wheat. Fat heads of garlic add the finishing touch to the arrangement.

Above: Space is often limited in a kitchen, so wall-mounted arrangements
such as this one are the perfect answer.

MATERIALS

Hanging baskets
SHALLOW BASKETS
DRY FOAM
FLORIST'S TAPE
SPHAGNUM MOSS
REEL WIRE
RAFFIA
PLANT MATERIAL
HYDRANGEA HEADS

Wall-mounted arrangement
WOODEN BOX (WALL MOUNTED)
DRY FOAM
STUB WIRE
PLANT MATERIAL
CENTAUREA, YELLOW
ACHILLEA, YELLOW
ALCHEMILLA, PALE YELLOW/GREEN
AMMOBIUM, WHITE
WHEAT HEADS, LIGHT BROWN
POPPY SEEDHEADS, LIGHT BROWN
GARLIC, CREAM
HARE'S TAIL GRASS, GREEN

Old clothes airers such as the one shown on the previous page can sometimes be found in antique shops, but modern reproductions are now available as well. Alternatively, suspend lengths of dowelling or bamboo poles from the ceiling (see page 34 for method). Tie the baskets to the poles with raffia or suspend them from metal butcher's hooks. When choosing baskets to hang up, remember that if the flowers are to be seen from below the basket will need to be fairly shallow – garden trugs and similar shapes are ideal. While you are filling the basket, hold it up from time to time in order to gauge the effect. For detailed instructions on how to make hanging bunches of dried flowers see pages 32–5.

The pine box is just one of a whole range of wall-mounted containers available to the dried-flower arranger. Alternatives include terracotta and stoneware planters, glazed pottery cornucopias and flat-backed baskets. Try to choose containers in keeping with the style of your kitchen: the pine box would be ideal with light wooden units, as would natural-weave baskets. Coloured glazed-pottery planters would be fine with painted or coloured units, and terracotta with darker shades of wood.

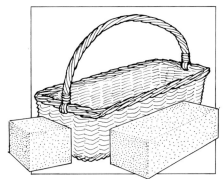

1 **For the hanging basket**, take a shallow basket such as a garden trug.

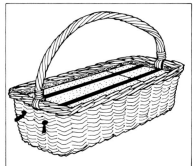

2 Cut pieces of dry foam to fit the basket, making sure that they do not sit higher than 2.5cm (1in) below the rim.

3 Tape the foam together, and fix into place by threading florist's tape through the sides of the basket. Cover with sphagnum moss.

4 Wire hydrangea heads and bunches of statice, and stick them firmly into the foam.

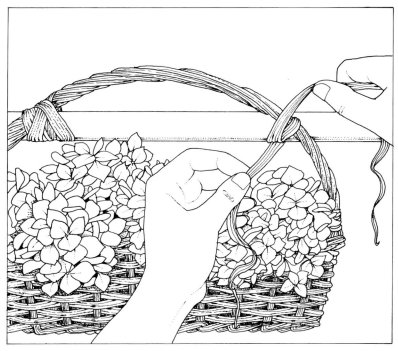

5 Attach the handle of the basket to the clothes airer with twists of raffia.

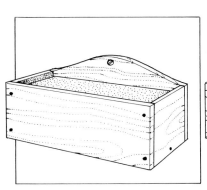

1 **The best way to make the wall-mounted arrangement** is to attach your container to the wall first and then construct the arrangement. If this is not possible, hold the arrangement up to the wall from time to time, so that you can see what it will look like when in place. Cut dry foam to fill the container and wedge it into place.

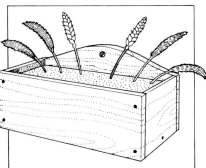

2 Start your design from the back, making a framework of wheat heads and poppy seedheads. Then work forwards and downwards.

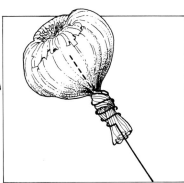

3 Finally, take garlic heads that still have some leaves on them. Twist the leaves together, wire, and fix into position.

versatile wreaths

Dried-flower wreaths make very effective and versatile decorations. The simple shape lends itself to all sorts of treatments and can be used in many ways throughout the house. Wreaths are also surprisingly easy to make, especially if you start with one of the many types of ready-prepared wreath base that are now available.

On the wreath in the picture opposite, the glowing colours of orange physalis and red helichrysum contrast with the green of wheat and the bright yellow achillea. Candles in the centre add a festive note: this would be a perfect dining-room decoration for an autumn or winter dinner party. Wreaths look equally good hung on the wall or on the back of a door, like the summery wreath of roses, hydrangea heads and peonies shown in the picture below.

Above: Decorate a cottage door with summer wreath of roses, hydrangeas
and peonies in pink, red and cream.

A number of different types of wreath base can be bought ready made from dried-flower stockists. These include circles of dry foam, plaited straw and raffia wreaths, and woven branches or vine stems. Wire frames which can be covered with moss are also available from florists (see page 24). It is not difficult to make your own wreath bases out of materials such as moss-filled wire mesh. For full instructions, see page 25.

The type of base chosen will be dictated by the style of the wreath. For example, a plaited straw wreath might be quite open in style, with much of the base showing between the flowers used to decorate it. Foam bases need to be well covered, so they will demand a closely packed arrangement of flowers.

The table wreath shown on the previous page is not made on a conventional wreath base. Instead, the dried material is glued around the rim of a shallow terracotta saucer. The centre of the bowl contains the candles, which are held in place with melted wax. The flower wreath base is made from wire mesh stuffed with moss. The roses, hydrangea heads and peonies for this wreath will need to be wired individually – see pages 22–4 for details.

1 | **To make the table wreath filled with candles**, begin by collecting together your materials. You will need to choose a shallow terracotta saucer – a large plant-pot base is ideal.

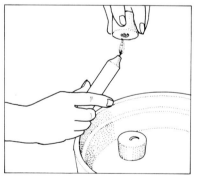

2 | Remove the night-light candles from their metal holders, melt the bases briefly in a candle flame and press them firmly on to the saucer. Do not position them too close to the rim or you risk setting fire to the wreath.

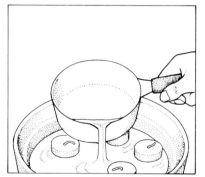

3 | Melt the large candles in a saucepan over a low heat. Pour the melted wax into the saucer, around the night-lights. Leave to set.

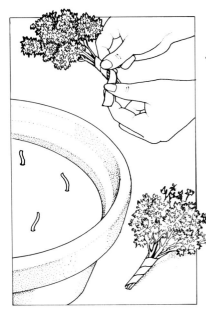

4 | Tape small bunches of alchemilla and glue them in pairs on to the inner and outer rims of the saucer.

5 | Tape bunches of green wheat and pink fescue grass and glue them on to the rim of the saucer.

6 | Add a mixture of physalis, achillea, helichrysum and carthamus seedheads.

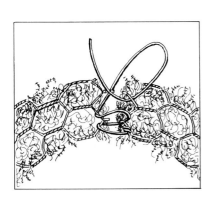

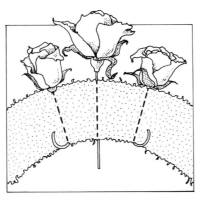

1 | **To make the flower wreath**, roll a 60cm (24in) length of wire mesh, 23cm (9in) wide, around a bundle of sphagnum moss, and wire the ends together.

2 | Attach wired rosebuds, peonies and hydrangea heads to the wreath, pushing the wired stems through the moss and bending round firmly.

3 | Tie a loop of cord or raffia around the wreath, leaving long ends for attaching the wreath to its support.

in the mood

The photographs on these pages show two very different styles of decoration, but both emphasize how effectively dried-flower arrangements can be used to highlight a decorative theme. The big arrangement in the picture opposite uses the bold shapes and textures of its exotic ingredients to make a very distinctive statement. Note how the rhythm of the design is dictated by the geometric shapes found in the oriental artefacts that surround it – the bamboo table, palm-leaf tray and split-cane blind. In complete contrast, the basket of dried barley in the picture below demonstrates the effectiveness of utter simplicity. It is a careful harmony of understated colours and shapes which makes an impact out of all proportion to its individual parts.

Above: Eyecatching groupings can be achieved in many different ways.
Here, two very different arrangements both make a big impact, thanks to
well-judged positioning and accessories.

MATERIALS

Seedhead basket

DEEP BASKET
NEWSPAPER
DRY FOAM
STUB WIRE
FLORIST'S TAPE
REEL WIRE

PLANT MATERIAL

ALLIUM SEEDHEADS, PALE GREEN
PALM FANS, PALE GREEN
FESCUE GRASS, PALE GREEN
BULRUSHES, LIGHT BROWN
LOTUS PODS, DARK BROWN
LOCUST BEANS, DARK BROWN
BRAZIL NUTS, BROWN
CONES, BROWN
DRIED FUNGI, BEIGE
CINNAMON STICKS, REDDISH
BROWN
HELICHRYSUM, CREAM/PINK
HELIPTERUM, CREAM
PROTEA, TAN/RUST

Barley basket

SHALLOW BASKET
RAFFIA OR CORD

PLANT MATERIAL

BARLEY

The angular shapes of the large arrangement shown on the previous page reflect the formal poses of oriental dancers like the one in the picture on the wall behind it. The clean lines of the seabird sculpture, on the other hand, make one think of an uncluttered landscape of sand dunes and sea grasses, which is reflected in the simplicity of the basket and its contents.

Taking a painting or a sculpture as inspiration for your dried-flower arrangements is an idea that has many different permutations. If you have a pretty flower print or painting on your wall, you might simply try to reproduce its shape and colours in dried flowers. Or you could, as here, use the painting to suggest a mood or a theme – autumn fruits and rich tones for an autumn landscape, for example; pale greens, blues and silvers for a sea theme; or bright blocks of colour for a vivid abstract.

The ingredients and style of the large arrangement suggest the orient, as many of them are grown in hot climates. The bold shapes come from lotus pods, palm fans, locust beans, Brazil nuts, cinnamon sticks, dried fungi, bulrushes, pink and green fescue grass and leucodendron, mixed with helichrysum, helipterum and allium heads.

1 **To make the large mixed arrangement**, start with a deep basket. A closely woven one is most suitable. Pad the base with crumpled paper.

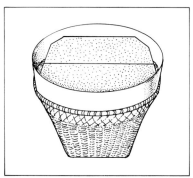

2 Cut blocks of dry foam to fit and wedge them into the top of the basket.

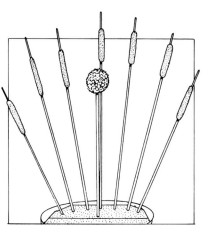

3 Use the bulrushes to create a fan shape. Then add the allium head. Place one large allium head in the centre as a focal point.

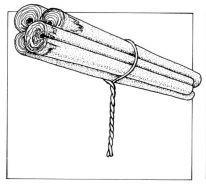

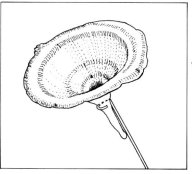

4 Wire the lotus pods, locust beans, Brazil nuts and dried fungi individually. Wire the cinnamon sticks into bundles. Wire stems of helichrysum and helipterum if they are not strong enough to stand upright.

5 Work forwards and outwards, adding the wired flowers and lotus pods, then the palm fans.

6 Once you have created the basic shape, add the remaining material, finishing with the cinnamon sticks at the base of the arrangement.

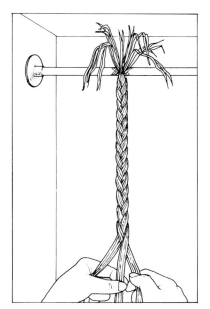

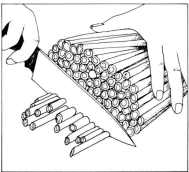

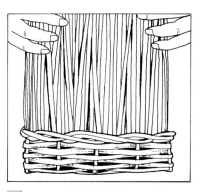

1 **The shallow side-table basket** uses a bunch of barley, bound with plaited cord. You could also use raffia.

2 Select a bunch of barley. The stalks should completely fill the base of the basket. Trim them evenly.

3 Plait lengths of cord or raffia and tie the plait firmly around the barley. Push the barley bunch into the basket, where it should stand upright. (If it does not, glue a thin layer of foam to the bottom of the basket and stick the barley stalks into it.)

bedroom posies

Think of dried-flower arrangements for the bedroom and the mind immediately springs to pretty bouquets in delicate pastel shades. The posies on these pages are certainly pretty enough for any bedroom, but they are very different from each other in mood, showing how easy it is to create variations on a single theme. The pink, lilac and cream posy in the photograph opposite, a charming traditional design, mixes glycerined rosebuds and carnations with silk flowers for a soft and very natural effect. The posy in the picture below, while equally attractive, has a bolder look with a more informal shape and stronger colours. The moss-filled basket is yet another idea for the bedroom – and can easily be moved if the surface on which it sits is needed for another purpose.

Above: A lacquer-red basket filled with moss and roses sits beside an informal posy of spring and summer flowers – two delightful flower decorations for any bedroom.

MATERIALS

Posies

STUB WIRE
REEL WIRE
COLOURED RIBBON
PLANT MATERIAL
GLYCERINED ROSEBUDS, PINK
SELECTION OF SILK FLOWERS IN
PINK, WHITE AND LAVENDER
(OR ANY THREE COLOURS AS
DESIRED)
GLYCERINED CARNATIONS,
PINK
SPRIGS OF ROSEMARY

Moss-filled basket

SMALL BASKET
SPRAY PAINT
BUN MOSS OR SPHAGNUM MOSS
AND DRY FOAM
PLANT MATERIAL
ROSEBUDS, WIRED

Posies like those shown on the previous pages are designed to be seen from the front and from above. They have a distinctive circular shape, gently rounded in front and flattened at the back. A formal posy is usually made up of rings of flowers in toning or contrasting colours; for ease of handling, small flowers will need to be wired into small bunches before the posy is made up. To create a less formal look, mix colours throughout the posy and add different textures, such as those of leaves, to give a variation in height. A ribbon bow gives a pretty finish and hides the wire around the stems.

The basket accompanying the informal posy is filled with bun moss with a ribbon of rosebuds running through the centre. Its simplicity is very effective, showing that there is no need to cram a container with flowers in order to make an impact. The basket is a plain wicker one, sprayed red. It is easy to spray baskets any colour you choose – see page 21 for details.

1 **In order to make a posy,** flowers need a good length of stem, so most will need to be wired, either individually or in small bunches.

2 For a formal design, start at the centre with a single flower or small bunch of flowers. Surround it with a circle of flowers in a contrasting colour.

3 Wire the flowers into place.

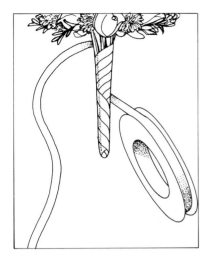

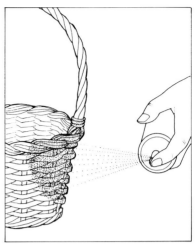

4 Continue to add more circles of flowers until you reach the size of posy that you require.

5 Wind coloured ribbon around the stem to hide the wiring, and finish with a bow. Leave the ends long.

1 **For the moss-filled basket,** first select a suitable basket and paint it the required colour – use a craft spray paint for the best results.

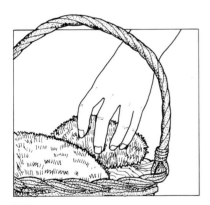

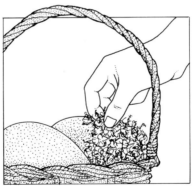

2 Take two mounds of bun moss and wedge them side by side in the basket.

3 If bun moss is not available, cut two mounds of foam, glue them into place and cover with sphagnum moss.

4 Take wired rosebuds and push them down between the mounds of moss to form a line. Make sure that the wires do not show.

conservatory flowers

It may seem perverse to consider decorating a conservatory with dried flowers, but these days the main function of many conservatories is as an extra room rather than as a home for delicate plants. Few except the dedicated gardener can spare the time and effort needed to look after a large collection of conservatory plants, so it makes sense to consider the decorative alternatives.

Tactfully used, dried flowers and plants can mingle happily with fresh ones, to give year-round colour and interest to the conservatory while cutting down on the work involved in plant maintenance. The key to successful arrangements is to keep them looking natural, like the grouping of dried flowers, seedheads and fresh berry trails on the wicker table opposite, artfully designed to look as if it has just been picked from the garden.

Above: A dried-flower tree in a vivid blue pot makes a brilliant splash of colour for a conservatory all year round.

Dried-flower tree
FLOWERPOT (PLASTIC OR
TERRACOTTA)
4–5 STRONG TWIGS
REEL WIRE
STUB WIRE
BLACK OR GREEN PLASTIC
PLASTER-OF-PARIS POWDER
DRY-FOAM BALL
SPHAGNUM MOSS
DECORATIVE CONTAINER

PLANT MATERIAL
AMMOBIUM
CORNFLOWERS
HELICHRYSUM
STATICE
POPPY SEEDHEADS
HONESTY SEEDPODS

Because the conservatory links outdoors and indoors, the best dried-flower arrangements to use here are informal. Keep the look as natural as possible, to blend with the live plants already growing in the conservatory and with the garden beyond the glass.

The grouping centred on the wicker table is carefully arranged to give the impression that the flowers and berries have just been picked from the garden and are drying naturally. The hydrangea heads and bunches of rosehips have been placed in containers without support and allowed to fall as they please. The containers themselves are stoneware in muted earth colours. Both wreaths are made on bases of twisted vines.

The head of the dried-flower tree is a ball of foam covered with moss. The stem is a bunch of twigs, set in a flowerpot filled with plaster of Paris. The flowerpot is then placed inside a decorative pot and hidden with moss or lichen. If, as here, the flowerpot is not to be seen, a plastic pot can be used. Otherwise, use a terracotta pot of appropriate size. The stems of the tree are wired to hold them together until the tree is finished, when they can be removed.

1 To make the dried-flower tree, first select your flowers. The tree uses a mix of ammobium, poppy seedheads, helichrysum, cornflowers and statice. Wire smaller flowers in small bunches, larger heads individually.

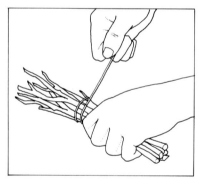

2 Select four or five sturdy twigs, such as hazel. Cut them to length (the height of the finished tree should not be more than three times the height of its pot) and wire them into a bundle.

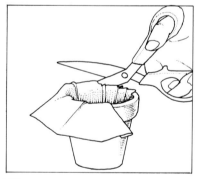

3 Line a plastic or terracotta flowerpot with plastic – use a piece cut from a green garden rubbish sack or bin liner.

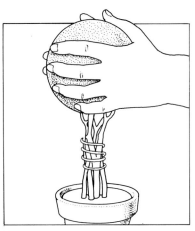

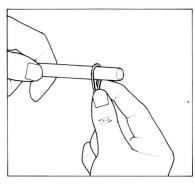

6 Cut short lengths of stub wire and bend them into the shape of hairpins to use as staples.

4 Mix plaster-of-Paris powder with water according to the manufacturer's instructions. Push the group of trunks into the pot and hold them in place as you spoon the plaster mix around. Allow to set.

5 Wedge a ball of dry foam – available ready-cut from dried-flower suppliers – on top of the twigs. Remove the wire around them.

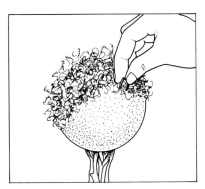

7 Use the wire staples to fix moss to the foam ball.

8 Push the wired flowers firmly into the foam, working around and around until the head of the tree is entirely covered.

9 Choose a suitable-sized container and place the tree in its pot inside. Fill the top of the container with a layer of moss to hide the base of the tree.

layered baskets

Most styles of dried-flower arrangement tend to be based on established ways of arranging fresh flowers, using a balance of shape, colour and texture to achieve a more or less natural look. The arrangements on these pages are different. Instead of trying to disguise the stiffness and immobility of dried flowers, they make a virtue of these attributes, using them to create eyecatching tiered stripes of colour.

Flat-backed arrangements like these are ideal for somewhere like a hall table, where they will be viewed from one side only. They make an immediate impact – important if they are only seen for a short time. In the picture opposite the stripes of colour are shown against neutral backgrounds, but they could equally well pick up the colours in carpet, tiles, wallpaper or curtains. This type of arrangement would also look very much at home filling a fireplace.

Above: Bold blocks of colour make an unusual variation on conventional dried-flower arrangements. This striking basket would be an eyecatcher wherever it were placed.

MATERIALS

Layered basket
LARGE RECTANGULAR BASKET OR
WOODEN BOX
DRY FOAM
GLUE
STUB WIRE
FLORIST'S TAPE

PLANT MATERIAL
AMARANTHUS, RED
WHEAT, GREEN
NIGELLA, PALE GREEN/BROWN
ALCHEMILLA, YELLOW/GREEN
HELICHRYSUM, YELLOW
LINUM (FLAX) SEEDHEADS, BROWN
HYDRANGEA HEADS, RED/GREEN
LAVENDER, BLUE

Baskets are ideal containers for tiered arrangements such as the one on the previous page. Try to choose a substantial basket with some weight to it, like the one shown in the picture, as a tall arrangement like this can be unstable. A lighter basket could be used, but it would need to be weighted. Any more-or-less rectangular container, such as a wooden box, would be a suitable alternative. Bear in mind that the arrangement should dominate the container and not vice-versa, so the container should have minimal decoration and be neutral or toning in colour.

At least some of the flowers and grasses will probably need to have their stems extended in order to provide enough height: see page 22 for instructions. They are then fixed into foam, which should be firmly wedged into place so that it is secure. For a permanent arrangement, it would be a good idea to glue the foam to the bottom of the basket. Begin with the tallest layer of flowers at the back and work forwards to the front, trimming the stems to ensure that the plants in each layer are of equal height. It may be helpful to lay out a selection of flowers in height order before you start work.

1 The flowers and plants used in the large tiered basket are hydrangea heads, helichrysum, nigella and linum seedheads, alchemilla, lavender, wheat and amaranthus.

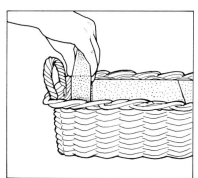

2 Cut pieces of foam to fit the rectangular basket and wedge or glue them into place.

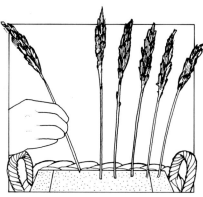

3 Begin with a row of amaranthus at what will be the back of the arrangement. These should form a gentle fan shape, with the highest point in the centre of the row.

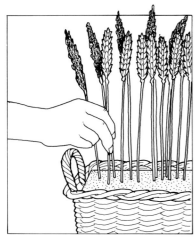

4 Fix a row of wheat in front of the amaranthus, with the stems close together.

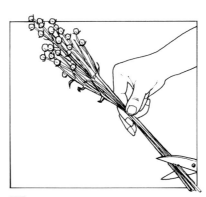

5 The third row is made up of linum seedheads, fixed into place in bunches. Trim the stems so that they are roughly equal in height.

6 Continue with a row of alchemilla. Curve this around the sides of the basket to hide the taller stems.

7 Next comes a row of lavender, again with the stems trimmed to equal lengths.

8 Wire the nigella seedheads into small bunches before using them to make the next row.

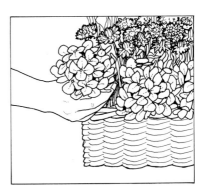

9 Wire the helichrysum into small bunches and the hydrangea heads singly, before fixing them into place for the final two rows.

flower trees

Dried-flower trees always make striking decorations, and can be used in many different areas of the house. A large, free-standing tree will fill many an awkward corner and smaller trees look equally good sitting on windowsills, table-tops or mantelpieces. Here are two styles of tree for two different settings. The three trees on the mantelpiece (opposite) are formal in mood. They are ideal for a sitting room decorated in traditional style, like this one with its striped wallpaper and Georgian-style fireplace surround. The single tree (below) is a looser style of arrangement. It would look good in a sitting room decorated in a more cottagey style, as suggested by the painted chest behind it and the flowered-print tablecloth on which it stands.

Above: Dried-flower trees can fit in anywhere, used either in a group or
singly, as shown here.

MATERIALS

Dried-flower trees

3 TERRACOTTA FLOWERPOTS
(GRADED SIZES)

3 LENGTHS OF WOOD

BLACK OR GREEN PLASTIC

PLASTER-OF-PARIS POWDER

3 DRY-FOAM BALLS
(GRADED SIZES)

REEL WIRE

STUB WIRE

LICHEN

GLUE

PLANT MATERIAL

AMMOBIUM, WHITE

HELICHRYSUM, RED

ACHILLEA, YELLOW

LAVENDER, BLUE

SEA HOLLY, BLUE

SEA LAVENDER, BLUE

STATICE, PURPLE

LINUM (FLAX) SEEDHEADS, BROWN

The trees shown on the previous pages are all built up around single balls of foam, but there is no need to limit yourself to one shape. Cone-shaped trees are very attractive and the foam cones are available from most dried-flower suppliers. You could also put two or more foam balls of different sizes on the same trunk, to imitate topiary. Or, for a simple tree, take a well-shaped, twiggy branch and plant it in a pot, glueing flowers on to the bare twigs.

The three trees grouped on the mantelpiece are permanently 'planted' in plaster of Paris in terracotta pots. If you wished to reuse the pots, smaller trees could be planted in sand instead. The plaster of Paris is hidden by lichen. Moss, pebbles, small flowerheads or pot-pourri could all be used as alternatives.

Note the height of the trees relative to their containers. Do not make the finished tree more than two-and-a-half to three times the height of its container or it will look top-heavy.

The single-stemmed trees use a mix of helichrysum, ammobium, statice, linum seedheads, sea holly, sea lavender, lavender and achillea. The multi-stemmed tree uses roses (dried in desiccant), and nigella seedpods (see page 27 for instructions for a multi-stemmed tree).

1 Select three terracotta pots of graded sizes and three straight lengths of wood.

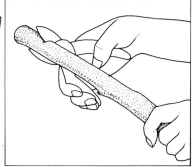

2 Cut each piece of wood to just over three times the height of each pot.

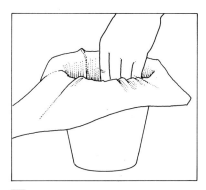

3 Line the pots with pieces of strong, dark-coloured plastic (e.g. from a refuse sack).

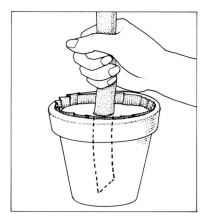

4 Fill the pots with plaster of Paris to about 2.5cm (1in) below their rims. Set the three stems firmly in the mixture. Leave to set.

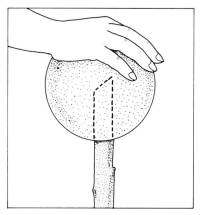

5 Take three balls of dry foam of graded sizes. Push one firmly on to the top of each stem.

6 Wire the smaller flowers with weak stems into bunches of five or six. Wire larger flowerheads individually if necessary.

7 Bend lengths of stub wire into staples. Use them to staple a layer of lichen on to each foam head.

8 Working all around the head, cover the lichen with flowers, pushing the stems firmly through into the foam.

9 Cover the base of each tree with a layer of lichen. A dab or two of glue will help to keep this in position.

finishing touches for the bedroom

Pretty dried-flower wreaths and garlands make ideal finishing touches for the bedroom. In the picture opposite, floral garlands are used as tie-backs for a pair of white muslin curtains to create a look that is both simple and sophisticated. The idea would work equally well with patterned curtains, if a single colour from the pattern was used for the flowers.

The big wreath in the picture below makes a lovely wall decoration, swathed in the same fabric as the cushion covers and with the colours picked out in the flowers as well. You could do the same with fabric from curtains, a tablecloth or a bedcover. Wreaths like this would also look good around mirrors or on the doors of dull cupboards or wardrobes.

Above: A sumptuous wreath is bound in fabric that matches the cushions on
a bedroom chair – a neat way to co-ordinate dried-flower decorations.

MATERIALS

Curtain tie-backs
2 × 60CM (24IN) LENGTHS OF
19MM (¾IN) WHITE BRAID OR
CORD
2 × 30CM (12IN) LENGTHS OF
6.4MM (¼IN) WHITE BRAID OR
CORD
REEL WIRE
FLORIST'S TAPE
GLUE OR GLUE GUN
PLANT MATERIAL
DELPHINIUMS, BLUE
HELICHRYSUM, CREAM/YELLOW
SEA LAVENDER, CREAM
DYED HARE'S TAIL GRASS HEADS,
RED

Fabric wreath
PLAITED-STEM WREATH BASE
FLOWER-PRINT FABRIC
REEL WIRE
STUB WIRE
FLORIST'S TAPE
PLANT MATERIAL
CLOVER, PINK
PEONIES, PINK
DYED HARE'S TAIL GRASS HEADS,
PINK
HELICHRYSUM, PINK
LARKSPUR, CREAM
AMARANTHUS, GREEN
HYDRANGEA HEADS, GREEN

Curtain tie-backs decorated with dried flowers look very pretty, but because the flowers are brittle and would be spoilt by regular handling, they are most practical when the curtains are not drawn every day – used in conjunction with a blind to keep out the light, for example. The base needs to be flexible so that it can loop around the curtains. Here, lengths of white braid are used to make the basic tie-back. The flowers are wired into small bunches, bound with green florist's tape and glued on to the braid. A hot-glue gun is useful for this fiddly work.

An alternative would be to make the tie-backs from lengths of plaited raffia or, for very light curtains, from plaited ribbon. Tie-backs in daily use could be decorated with a single posy of flowers, instead of all along their length. The flowers used here are helichrysum, sea lavender, delphiniums, and dyed hare's tail grass heads.

The bedroom wreath is constructed on a base of plaited vine stems. The length of fabric is wrapped around the wreath and glued into position before the flowers are attached. The flowers are dyed grass heads, larkspur, amaranthus, clover, hydrangea heads and peonies.

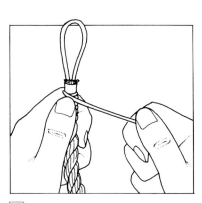

1 **For the curtain tie-backs**, take two 60cm (24in) lengths of white braid. Use two narrower lengths of braid to form loops and bind on to the ends.

2 Divide the flowers into small bunches of different colours and trim the stems.

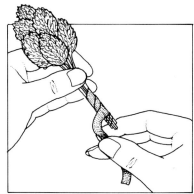

3 Wire each bunch and bind the stem with green florist's tape.

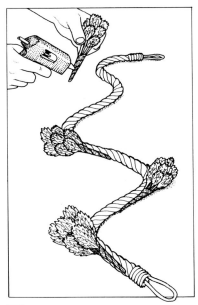

4 Glue the flower bunches carefully on to the braid.

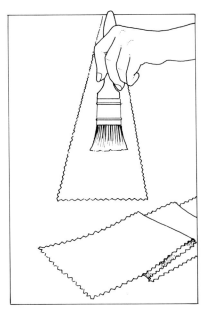

1 **To make the fabric wreath**, cut a piece of flower-print fabric approximately long enough to wind around the wreath four times. Cut a second length for the bow.

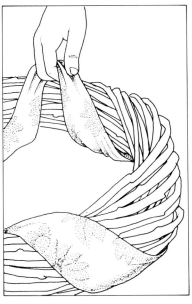

2 Paste glue on to the back of the length of cloth to be wound around the wreath. Bind the cloth around the wreath and press into place. Leave the glue to dry.

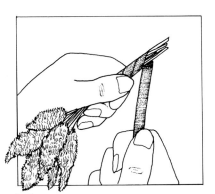

3 Shorten the stems of the flowers and wire them singly or in small bunches, depending on size. Bind with florist's tape.

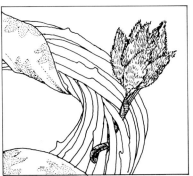

4 Attach the flowers to the wreath between the fabric, pushing the stems through the wreath and bending them back. A dab of glue will help to keep them in place.

5 Tie the remaining length of cloth into a bow and wire it to the wreath.

flowers for special occasions

From time to time there are occasions when you will wish to make the house look really special – at Christmas perhaps, or for a wedding, anniversary celebration or any other party. Here dried flowers really come into their own, because you can organize the decorations well in advance and then forget about them. Fresh flowers are lovely, of course, but to ensure that they look their best you must leave everything until the last minute, when there are always masses of other things to do. In the picture opposite, classic Christmas swags of dried pine branches and gilded cones flank a roaring log fire. Swags like these would look equally good around a mirror, looped through the banisters or over a mantelpiece or door lintel. In contrasting summery mood, the flower-garland table shown in the picture below is ideal for a wedding party.

Above: Festive swags and garlands spell celebration all year round. A summery bridal garland sets the scene for a garden wedding reception.

Festive swag
GOLD SPRAY PAINT
SMALL-GAUGE WIRE MESH
STUB WIRE
REEL WIRE
GLUE OR GLUE GUN
WIDE GOLD RIBBON

PLANT MATERIAL
OAK LEAVES, BROWN (GILDED)
PECAN OR BRAZIL NUTS, BROWN
(GILDED)
PINE CONES, BROWN (GILDED)
POPPY SEEDHEADS, LIGHT BROWN
PINE BRANCHES, GREEN

The bridal table is covered with a muslin cloth on top of a cotton cloth. The muslin is pinned to suggest the folds of a bridal gown, then nails are driven into the table at intervals to support the garland. The garland mixes good-quality fabric flowers with the dried flowers. This is a good idea if you want to match a particular colour that cannot be found in dried flowers, and often looks more natural than using dried flowers which have been dyed.

The base of the garland is wire mesh stuffed with moss. Lighter garlands can be created simply by fixing wired bunches of flowers together along a length of reel wire, or by wiring them on to a length of cord. Alternatively, there are now ready-made garland bases available, constructed from blocks of foam in linked plastic 'cages'.

The Christmas swag is made on a base of wire mesh, into which gold-sprayed leaves, cones and seedheads are inserted. The swag shown on the previous page uses fresh pine foliage, which will dry in place. The ornamental angel is optional – the bow would look equally good on its own. When making up the swag, work with it flat on the table, but hold it up from time to time so that you can assess the effect.

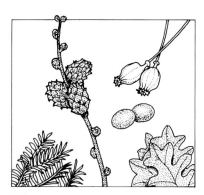

1 For the swag, collect together pine branches, pine cones still attached to their twigs, glycerined oak leaves, poppy seedheads, pecan or Brazil nuts, gold spray paint, ribbon and wire mesh.

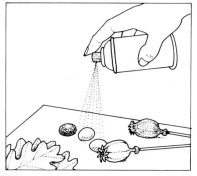

2 Spray the oak leaves, nuts, pine cones and poppy seedheads gold.

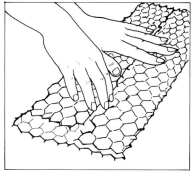

3 Take a rectangular piece of small-gauge wire mesh, the same length as the swag you require and twice the width. Bend each side to the middle, forming a double layer.

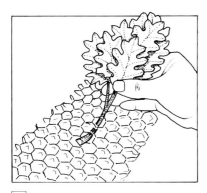

4 Fix the oak leaves into place first, pushing the stems through the wire mesh.

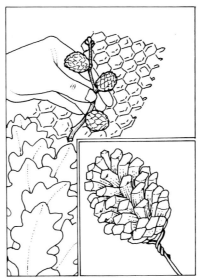

5 Add the pine cones on their twigs. Any loose cones can be wired into place. To wire a cone (inset), take a length of stub wire and twist it around the cone above the lowest layer of scales.

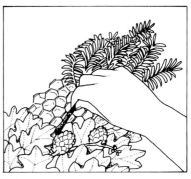

6 Fix the pine branches into place between the sprayed material, making sure that the wire mesh is well hidden.

7 Glue the gold-sprayed nuts on to the pine foliage.

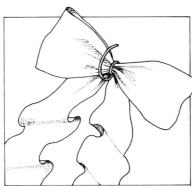

8 Make up a double bow of wide gold ribbon.

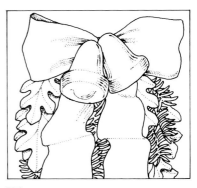

9 Wire the ribbon bow to the top of the swag. Add an ornament such as an angel or bell, if liked. The wire mesh backing of the swag can easily be hooked over a nail to fix the swag securely to the wall.

FLOWERS AND PLANTS
FOR DRYING

Today, dried flowers are readily available from many sources. However, if you grow and dry your own you will both save money and build up a more varied and interesting range of material for your arrangements.

Some of the most popular and useful dried flowers are annuals, which can be grown easily from seed. These include the true everlasting flowers such as helichrysum, statice, ammobium and xeranthemum. Many garden perennials are also good for drying – achillea, astrantia, alchemilla, larkspur, gypsophila and sea holly, for example – while shrubs and trees can provide both leaves and seedheads.

There are also increasing numbers of specialist growers who will let you harvest your own flowers for drying, as well as sell you ready-dried flowers. They normally have a good range of flowers from which to choose, and you can select the best specimens in peak condition.

The following list gives details of a selection of the best flowers and plants to grow and/or dry yourself. However, it is by no means exhaustive, and it is well worth experimenting with other garden plants and flowers.

Acanthus mollis (bear's breeches)
Perennial
Tall white-and-purple flower spikes. *A. spinosus* has shorter spikes. Air dry, hanging upside-down.

Acer (maple)
Tree
Most maples have beautiful autumn colour. Pick sprays as the leaves begin to turn and press them under a rug or carpet. Maple leaves can also be preserved in glycerine.

Achillea (yarrow)
Perennial
Most achilleas dry well. Try *A. filipendulina* 'Gold Plate', with flat heads of yellow flowers; *A. ptarmica* 'The Pearl', with clusters of small white flowers; and *A. millefolium* varieties such as the pink 'Cerise Queen'. Air dry, hanging upside-down.

Aconitum napellus (monkshood)
Perennial
Deep blue flower spikes. For best results, pick before the flowers are fully open. All parts of this plant are *poisonous* – handle with care. Air dry, hanging upside-down.

Acroclinum roseum (sunray)
Annual
Daisy-like flowers in pink, white and red, with black or yellow centres. Easy to dry. Air dry, hanging upside-down.

Alchemilla mollis (lady's mantle)
Perennial
Clusters of tiny, greenish yellow flowers. Pick as soon as the flowers are open for best colour. Air dry, hanging upside-down.

Allium (ornamental onion)
Bulb
There are several ornamental alliums that can be dried either as flowers or seedheads. The flowers are white, pink or pale purple. Air dry, hanging upside-down.

Althea rosea (hollyhock)
Biennial
Tall spikes of single or double flowers in a wide range of colours. Pick before the flowers are fully open. Air dry, hanging upside-down.

Amaranthus caudatus (love-lies-bleeding)
Annual
A striking plant with hanging tassels of deep red flowers. Air dry, upright.

Amaranthus paniculatus
Annual
Upright red or green flower spikes. Air dry, hanging upside-down.

Ambrosinia mexicana
Annual
Tall green flower spikes. Air dry, hanging upside-down.

Ammobium alatum (winged everlasting)
Annual
Small, daisy-like white flowers. A true everlasting: pick just before the flowers open fully. Air dry, hanging upside-down.

Anaphalis margaritacea (pearl everlasting)
Annual
Grey foliage and small white flowers with yellow centres. Air dry, hanging upside-down.

Anaphalis triplinevsis (snowy everlasting)
Annual
Small white flowers and grey foliage. Air dry, hanging upside-down.

Anethum graveolens (dill)
Annual herb
If dill is allowed to flower it produces attractive yellow-green flowerheads, similar to cow parsley. Dry flowers or seedheads. Air dry, hanging upside-down.

Arctotis grandis (African daisy)
Annual
Showy daisy flowers in white, pink, red and orange. Useful for large arrangements. Air dry, hanging upside-down.

Astilbe × arendsii (astilbe)
Perennial
Tall flower spikes in white to pink and deep red. Pick as the flowers begin to open. Air dry, hanging upside-down.

Astrantia major (masterwort)
Perennial
Delicate, papery flowers with pink or greenish white petals. Easy to dry. Pick when flowers have just opened. Air dry, hanging upside-down.

Atriplex hortensis (orach)
Annual
Tall green or red seed spikes. Air dry, hanging upside-down.

Avena sativa (oats)
Grass
Harvest while the heads are still green, or allow to ripen to gold. Air dry, hanging upside-down.

Betula pendula (silver birch)
Tree
The heart-shaped leaves with their silver undersides can be preserved in glycerine.

Briza maxima (quaking grass)
Grass
A grass with distinctive drooping clusters of seedheads. Pick before the seeds are ripe. Air dry, upright or hanging upside-down.

Buddleia davidii (butterfly bush)
Shrub
Spikes of tiny florets in white or shades of blue, lavender and purple. Pick as soon as the flowers have opened, or allow seedheads to dry on the plant. Air dry, hanging upside-down.

Carthamus tinctorius (safflower)
Annual
Handsome green, thistle-like heads with tufted centres in bright orange. Pick as green buds or when the orange is just showing. Air dry, hanging upside-down.

Centaurea cyanus (cornflower)
Annual
Pretty white, pink and blue flowers that are ideal for smaller arrangements. Pick just as the flowers open. Air dry, hanging upside-down.

Centaurea macrocephala (knapweed)
Perennial
Thistle-like yellow heads. Pick as soon as the flowers start to open or leave for seedheads. Air dry, hanging upside-down.

Clematis
Perennial climber
A big family of climbers, useful for their fluffy seedheads. Lengths of the twisting stems can also be used for wreaths and garlands. Twist stems into

the desired shape while still green. Air dry, hanging upside-down.

Cortaderia selbana (pampas grass)
Grass
This tall grass has distinctive tufted cream heads, ideal for very large arrangements. Pick before the heads are fully open to avoid shedding. Air dry, upright.

Calluna vulgaris (heather)
Shrub
Delicate mauve, pink or white bells. Air dry, upright.

Craspedia globosa (drumstick)
Annual
Tightly packed round heads of small yellow flowers on long stems. Air dry, upright.

Cynara cardunculus (cardoon)
Perennial
Large thistle-like heads, similar to those of an artichoke, with tufted purple centres. Pick as soon as the purple tuft begins to appear or leave for seedheads. Air dry, upright with the head supported.

Delphinium consolida (larkspur)
Annual
An excellent flower for drying. Tall spikes in white, pinks and blues. Air dry, hanging upside-down.

Delphinium elatum (delphinium)
Perennial
Available in a wide range of shades including white, pink, red, blues and purples. Pick the flower spikes before the top buds have opened fully. Air dry, hanging upside-down.

Echinops ritro (globe thistle)
Perennial
Round steel-blue flowerheads and grey, thistle-like leaves. Pick as soon as the heads start to colour, before the flowers are fully open. Air dry, hanging upside down.

Ergyngium (sea holly)
Perennial
The spiky silver or silvery blue flowerheads are an interesting shape, with prickly grey-green foliage. Pick as soon as the heads have coloured, or leave to ripen on the plant. Air dry, upright or hanging upside-down.

Euphorbia (spurge)
Perennial
There are many different varieties of euphorbia, with striking heads made up of bright green or yellow bracts. *E. griffithii* 'Fireglow' has bright red bracts – pick as soon as the bracts are coloured. Handle all types carefully, as the sticky sap from the stems can irritate the skin. Air dry, hanging upside-down.

Eucalyptus (gum tree)
Tree
The most useful varieties of eucalyptus for the dried-flower arranger have silver or grey-green leaves. The young foliage dries best. Air dry, hanging upside-down, or preserve in glycerine (this will turn the leaves a darker colour).

Fagus sylvatica (beech)
Tree
The fresh green foliage can be preserved in glycerine, where it will turn a rich brown, or the leaves can be allowed to dry on the plant and used as they are. Copper beech is a deep purple-brown.

Gomphrena globosa (globe amaranth)
Annual
Pink and white clover-like blossoms. Pick as soon as flowers are fully formed. Air dry, hanging upside-down.

Gypsophila paniculata (Baby's breath)
Perennial
Airy sprays of delicate white flowers on branching stems. Air dry, hanging upside-down.

Helichrysum bracteatum (strawflower)
One of the most useful everlasting flowers and easy to grow, in a wide variety of good colours from white through yellows and oranges to pink and deep red. There are several species of helichrysum, all of which dry well. Pick before the flowers are fully open and air dry, hanging upside-down.

Helipterum manglesii (Swan River daisy)
Annual
Daisy-like flowers with papery pink or white petals. Air dry, hanging upside-down.

Helleborus niger (Christmas rose)
Perennial
Beautiful single white flowers, which can be preserved in desiccant. The dark green leaves also press well. The flowers of *H. orientalis* hybrids (Lenten rose) in creams and purples can also be dried in desiccant.

Heuchera (coral flower)
Perennial
Sprays of small white, pink or red bell-shaped flowers on long, curved stems. Air dry, upright.

Humulus lupulus (hop)
Perennial climber
Green cone-shaped flowers (female plants only). The long, twining stems are excellent for garlands. Do not pick until the flowers are fully developed. Air dry, suspended horizontally. Twine the hop step around a cane or pole for support.

Hydrangea macrophylla (mophead hydrangea)
Shrub
Hydrangeas dry very well. Colours range from white to pinks, reds, blues and green. Cut in the autumn, when the heads are fully mature. Air dry, upright or hanging upside-down. Hydrangeas can also be preserved in glycerine.

Lavandula spica (lavender)
Perennial
Lavenders are excellent for drying, especially those in darker shades of mauve or purple. Choose types with long flower spikes, such as 'Hidcote Giant', and cut before the buds open. Air dry, hanging upside-down.

Limonium latifolium (sea lavender)
Perennial
Arching sprays of delicate pale mauve or white flowers that are very easy to dry. Air dry, hanging upside-down.

Limonium sinuatum (statice)
Annual
Very useful and easy to dry in a wide range of colours: pink, blue, white, purple and yellow. A true everlasting. Air dry, hanging upside down.

Lonas inodora (African daisy)
Annual
Round, bright yellow flowers, good for small arrangements. Air dry, hanging upside-down.

Lunaria (honesty)
Biennial
The round, silvery seedpods of this mauve- or white-flowered biennial are useful in many arrangements. Pick while the pods are still green, or leave them on the plant until autumn to ripen and turn silver. Air dry, hanging upside-down.

Molucella laevis (bells of Ireland)
Annual
Unusual greenish bell-shaped flowers in whorls around a central stem. Pick as soon as the lower bells have opened. Air dry, hanging upside-down.

Nicandra physaloides (shoo-fly plant)
Annual
Pale green seedheads, similar to Chinese lanterns (*Physalis*). Air dry, upright or hanging upside-down.

Nigella damascena (love-in-a-mist)
Annual
The pretty pink, blue or white flowers can be dried, but the striped seedheads are the most useful part of the plant. Pick when green, or leave to dry naturally on the plant. Air dry, hanging upside-down.

Paeonia (peony)
Perennial
Beautiful single or double flowerheads in pinks, white and reds. Not easy to dry, but very effective if successful. Cut before the flowers are fully open. Hang in small bunches in a warm, dry place or preserve individual flowerheads in desiccant.

Papaver (poppy)
Annual/Perennial
Many poppies have attractive seedheads, especially *P. somniferum* (opium poppy). Pick while the pods are still green. Air dry, hanging upside-down.

Physalis (Chinese lantern)
Perennial
The bright orange seedpods are good in autumn or winter arrangements. Pick as soon as the pods are fully coloured. Air dry, upright.

Quercus robur (oak)
Tree
Oak leaves turn a rich red-brown when preserved in glycerine. Pick the leaves when they are fully mature.

Rosa (rose)
Shrub
The easiest roses to dry are the long-stemmed varieties with small, tightly furled heads. Cut them when the buds are just beginning to open. Sprays of rosehips from species roses such as *R. moyesii* and *R. glauca* may be picked in the autumn. Individual rose flowers of many varieties can be dried in desiccant. Red roses hold their colour best. Air dry, hanging upside-down.

Salvia horminum (clary)
Annual
The spikes of cream, pink or purple bracts should be picked when fully coloured. Air dry, hanging upside-down.

Santolina (cotton lavender)
Shrub
Small yellow flowers and grey foliage. Pick as soon as the flowers are open. Air dry, hanging upside-down.

Solidago (golden rod)
Perennial
Tall spires of bright yellow flowers. Pick as soon as the first flowers have opened and while the top of the flower spike is still green. Air dry, hanging upside-down.

Viburnum tinus (laurustinus)
Shrub
The shiny dark green foliage of this evergreen shrub can be preserved in glycerine.

Xeranthemum annuum (everlasting flower)
Annual
Daisy-like double flowers in white and shades of pink and purple. Air dry, hanging upside-down.

DRYING TECHNIQUES

There are three main ways of preserving the flowers and plants that you have picked or grown yourself. These are: air drying (the easiest and most popular method); the use of desiccants such as silica gel, sand or borax; and glycerining. A fourth method of preserving flowers is by pressing. Normally, pressing does not produce specimens suitable for dried-flower arrangements, but it can sometimes be successful with leaves and ferns.

To achieve a successful end result when drying flowers, you must start with the right material, harvested under the right conditions. Pick flowers just before they come into full bloom: if allowed to open completely, their colours will start to fade and they will tend to shed their petals as they dry. Some flowers, such as roses, dry well in the bud stage. Cut grasses as soon as the seedheads are fully formed. Pick deciduous leaves for glycerining when they are mature, but before they begin to take on their autumn colour.

Always pick on a dry day, when any dew has disappeared. If you pick when it is damp, the plants may develop mildew. After picking, sort through the plants. Remove grubs and insects and any fading or damaged flowers, and thin out overcrowded stems.

AIR DRYING

Air drying is the best way of preserving most flowers and plants, as long as the right drying conditions can be provided. The ideal spot is dry, airy, dark and not too cool. Flowers will fade rapidly in bright light, and will go mouldy in cold, damp places. Airing cupboards, attics, spare room, or, in warmer climates, sheds and garages can all be suitable – a few experiments will quickly show you the best location in your own home.

Hanging bunches

First remove any surplus leaves, and then tie the flower stems together in bunches of six to 12, depending on the size of the flowerheads. Arrange the bunches so that the flowerheads are at different levels to prevent them being crushed. Use elastic bands, string or raffia to hold the stems together and hang the bunches at least 15cm (6in) apart so that the air can circulate around them. Check the stems for shrinkage from time to time as they dry, and tighten the fastenings as necessary.

Drying times vary from plant to plant and depend on drying conditions. Some flowers may take only a week, others a month or more. They are ready when the flowerheads, leaves and stems are dry right through with no trace of moisture left, and the whole plant has a papery feel to it.

Drying upright

Some plants dry best in an upright position, especially taller items such as grasses. Trim the stems and stand the plants upright in a container such as a vase or large jar.

Drying on a rack

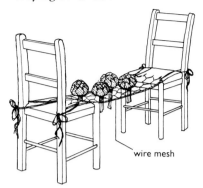

wire mesh

Heavy-headed plants such as globe artichokes and large thistles may need their heads supported as they dry. A piece of wire mesh, supported on two chairs, is ideal for this. Push each stem down through the wire until the head is resting on the mesh, and then leave to dry in the normal way.

Drying in water

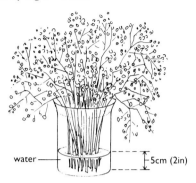

water — 5cm (2in)

Flowers like hydrangeas, heathers and gypsophila benefit if the drying process is started with their stems in water. Pour about 5cm (2in) depth of water into a large vase or jar and stand the flowers in it. Allow the water to dry up, and then leave the flowers to dry in the normal way.

DESICCANTS

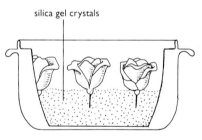

silica gel crystals

When drying flowers, the most lifelike results are achieved through the use of desiccants like silica gel, sand and borax. Desiccants work by absorbing moisture from the plant, leaving it dry and brittle but preserving both shape and colour very effectively. This is not a method for bulk production of dried material, but is ideal for choice flowers such as roses and peonies.

1 The best desiccant is silica gel. Silica gel crystals are expensive to buy, but can be reused almost indefinitely. Pour a layer of crystals into a lidded container such as an old biscuit tin or ice-cream carton. Then lay the flowers, facing upwards, on top, making sure that they do not touch each other. It is a good idea to give each flower a short wire stem (see page 22), as this will make it easier to handle when dry.

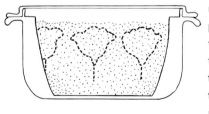

2 Carefully spoon more crystals around, into and over each flower, making sure that the petals aren't crushed in the process. When the flowers are completely covered,

replace the lid of the container and place it in a warm, dry place. Leave for two days, then check carefully to see if the flowers are dry. If they are not, leave for another day. Once dry, store the flowers in an airtight container to prevent them reabsorbing moisture from the air.

Used silica gel crystals can be dried for reuse. Spread them out on a tray and dry in a medium oven for about one hour, then store in an airtight container.

GLYCERINE

Some plant material, especially leaves, can be preserved by glycerining, which replaces the natural moisture in the plant with a solution of glycerine and water. Most glycerined plants turn brown, but the colours can be very attractive, ranging from pale fawn through rich tan virtually to black.

Oak, beech, eucalyptus, maple and magnolia leaves are those most commonly preserved in glycerine solution, but it is worth experimenting with other foliage. Use only mature leaves – the glycerine treatment is not effective on young foliage.

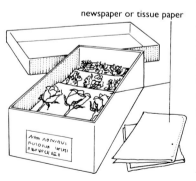

glycerine — 10cm (4in)

Strip the lower leaves off the foliage and crush the bases of the stems. Mix glycerine with the same volume of very hot water and stir well. Pour the solution into a jar or vase and stand the prepared stems in it – the liquid should come about 10cm (4in) up the stem. A glass jar will enable you to monitor the level of the solution and top it up as necessary. Place the jar in a dark place and leave the foliage in the solution until the whole leaf has changed colour. This may take a week or longer.

PRESSING

Ferns and large sprays of foliage can be dried by pressing. Even though flat, they will still be useful as background material for swags or larger arrangements. Lay the leaves on a double thickness of newspaper, place a couple more sheets of newspaper on top, and place them under a heavy rug or carpet, preferably where they will not be walked on too often. They should dry in about four weeks.

STORAGE

If you have the space, dried flowers can be stored as hanging bunches. Otherwise, the best method of storage is to pack the flowers in large cardboard boxes – these are often available from florists.

newspaper or tissue paper

Pack the flowers in layers, with sheets of newspaper or tissue paper between them. Do not overfill the boxes, or the flowers may be crushed. Label the boxes with their contents, so that you can keep track of your stock. Make sure that the boxed flowers are stored in a dry place, or they may develop mildew.

If flowers and leaves are crushed during storage, they can sometimes be revived by steaming. Hold them in the steam from a pan of boiling water for a short while, and then gently push them back into shape.

Flowers preserved in silica gel should be stored in airtight containers with a few silica gel crystals to absorb any moisture.

INDEX

Page numbers in *italic* refer to the illustrations